A FAMILY HARVEST

A FAMILY HARVEST

by Jane Moss Snow

BEING THE RECIPES AND RECORD
OF GOOD EATING
FROM THE SHORES OF MARYLAND
AND THE ROCKY BERKSHIRES
OF MASSACHUSETTS

BOBBS-MERRILL

Indianapolis/New York

Library of Congress Cataloging in Publication Data

Snow, Jane Moss.
    A family harvest.

        1. Cookery, American—Maryland.   2. Cookery,
American—Massachusetts.   I. Title.
TX715.S676   641.5′9744′1   75-33569
ISBN 0-672-52169-5

Designed by Betty Crumley
Manufactured in the United States of America

First printing

To my most beloved husband and mother

whose patience made this book possible

Contents

VEGETABLES   88

Fried apples • Broccoli Maryland • Creamed celery • Corn on the cob • Southern fried corn • Corn pudding I • Corn pudding II • Succotash • Cabbage and cornmeal dumplings • Eggplant—baked, fried or broiled • Greens —turnip, collard and kale • Baked onions • Boiled okra • Okra and tomatoes • Okra and string beans • Fresh peas and dumplings • Stuffed peppers • Sautéed sweet potatoes • Orange sweet potatoes • Candied sweet potatoes • Escalloped potatoes • Mosie's baked squash • Mom Bradley's sautéed squash • The fresh tomato • Stewed tomatoes • Baked tomatoes • Fried tomatoes • Baked stuffed tomatoes • Tomato aspic • Yellow turnips (rutabagas) • Slaw and dressing

HOMINY, GRITS AND SOUFFLÉS   110

Hominy • Grits • Fried grits • Baked grits • Gnocchi à la Lorraine • Laurena's cheese soufflé • Lois' dependable cheese soufflé

BREADS AND GRIDDLE CAKES   116

Cornbread • Cornsticks • Spoonbread • Johnnycake • Ann Sands' pone bread —1835 • Our white bread • Grandmother's rolls • Sweet potato bread • Banana bread • Snow's graham nut bread • Aunt Cretia's rolled oats bread • Jean Snow's date nut bread • Boston brown bread • Soft gingerbread • Pork cake • Buttermilk biscuits • Maryland beaten biscuits • Sweet potato biscuits • Our muffins—plain, blueberry and raisin • Cornmeal muffins • Our raised muffins • Whole wheat popovers • Aunt Janie Revell's rice pone • Fritters— vegetable and fruit • Grandmother Clary's cornmeal griddle cakes with maple syrup • Cornmeal griddle cakes—southern Maryland style • Breadcrumb griddlecakes • Rice griddle cakes • Cheese wafers

STUFFINGS   142

Bread stuffing • Oyster stuffing • Crab stuffing

PICKLES AND CONSERVES   145

Ann Sands' pickling instructions—1836 • Grandmother's mustard pickles • Bread and butter pickles • Pin money pickles • Sweet pickle watermelon rind • Ripe tomato pickle • Piccalilli • Aunt Fanny's pepper relish • Pepper hash • Chili sauce • Rhubarb relish • Frances Snow's yellow tomato conserve •

Introduction

In this day of migrating society, when families are as dispersed as the seven tribes of Israel, the traditions of the kitchen are being lost and forgotten along with last year's tennis shoes. My generation, which matured after the Second World War, may be the last to have savored food prepared in virtually the same way by the same recipes that had been used from the 18th century.

When I was a child, my grandparents' homes were the most stable element in my life. It was simply that they were there, in the same spot, unchanging, the shaded stillness of the Annapolis house waiting to be cracked by our arrival shouts, then mended afresh with the ensuing hushes.

In the summer we stayed at the Bay Ridge house down where the Severn meets the Chesapeake, while my grandparents stayed in town. It was at Bay Ridge that I became conscious of a garden. I planted my first cantaloupe seed while the Bob White called me from the brush. It was there that I fell heir to the onerous task of shredding the cabbage for slaw until it was as fine as the knife blade itself.

And it was there beside the bottomless black of Cat Hole that I learned the secret of netting the crab by keeping the fall of my shadow away from the water while holding my breath, lest either sight or sound frighten the creature away.

The Moss family has been nurtured by the shores of the Chesapeake for some 350 years, living off the succulents of the land and the water. The marshes harbored the shedding crab. The oysters were raked off the bay bottom. The growing season was long and slow and hot, forcing the land to heave forth its varied succession of fruits and vegetables.

Long after most of the nation had settled for vegetables picked while green and ripened in refrigerator cars as they were sped to market, my grandfather still tilled his little garden, continuing until his 84th year.

He never thought anything worth eating that hadn't been freshly picked or caught, and belabored the science that had hybridized the goodness out of the seeds of life.

His delight when gruffly announcing that the first string beans would be ready the next day was only equalled by the spying of the shad trees flowering or the sight of the first skipjack docking with its decks piled from gunn'l to gunn'l with Carolina watermelons.

Ah, but that was great excitement for a child . . . springing aboard, going through the mysterious thumpings of the melons until the juiciest thump was discovered. And how I looked forward to that sweet pickled rind!

It was at least 1950 before I discovered as a new bride that most of the dishes I loved and wanted to make existed only in someone's mind. Mother had begun writing down some of her mother's and grandmother's recipes when she was married in 1919, but she, too, had learned by watching and doing, really cooking by instinct as generations had done before her.

Certain recipes had become specialties with individuals and were remembered only by them. I often found myself with one hand stirring the pot, while I dialed my mother frantically halfway across the country to ask what to do next, only to hear her say: "That's a recipe I don't know. You'll have to ask Bong."

Through the years, I gradually accumulated a store of old recipes. Sometimes there would be three versions of the same one: my mother's, my aunt Bong's and my aunt Beppy's, all based on my grandmother's or great-grandmother's.

And practically all of them were without measurements and often omitted ingredients which I was supposed to know about automatically. Suddenly I realized the clock was running and no one had compiled these wonderful old recipes.

Thus was this book conceived.

The earliest written recipes in my family are those of Ann Sands, who began a reference of sorts in 1835. Paper must have been scarce, as she used her papa's 1779 ledger books, pasting homilies, poems, recipes, hints for the care of the skin and all matter of things over his carefully written accounts. Although our family records are among the most comprehensive in Maryland, the cookbooks, if they existed, were apparently destroyed in various fires and even thrown away as great, great Aunt Mary did with hers in a cleaning fit at the age of 90 or thereabouts.

And so most of these recipes are written here for the first time, although their origins can be traced for generations.

This began as a Southern Maryland family recipe book, but it seemed a shame to ignore the hundred years of fragments of recipes still in the Snow family.

Like the Mosses, the Snows no longer have their lands and homes, but are scattered into today with no central hearth. Snow traditions are even more threatened than ours, as there has been no "handing down" for two generations. The recipes I have been able to resurrect are those given me by Frances Clary Snow, my husband's mother, the last of the family who knew how things had been. The written ones date back to a tiny notebook of her mother's from 1876, helping to form a fascinating commentary on New England farm life, so different from that of the Maryland shore.

Snow Farm was a little world in itself, ranging up to the top of the mountain, stretching its way across the face. Settled on a small green plateau about a mile up was the old New England Federal house, its earthy brick square attached to the original 1713 wooden farmhouse that now forms the dining room, kitchen, borning room, and the children's and hired man's bedrooms.

Old and gnarled maples spread over it protectively. The arbutus joyfully framed the green clearing, sprawling riotously down the bank of the stream. The house had gradually shifted and settled with the rhythms of the earth until it echoed the subtle meandering of the land.

The mountain mothered the family, giving of its fruits and sap and berries in return for the droppings of the herds and the tilling of its fields. The sugar maples opened their veins in the spring. The wild bees led the way to their honeycombs. The orchards dropped their prizewinning apples beginning with the

Yellow Transparents in July and continuing through to the reddening of the McIntosh in September, ready to be laid down with the turnips and potatoes in the cold cellar.

The craggy ledges were thorned with blueberries, blackberries, raspberries. The lady slipper and lobelia seeds were gathered and pulverized with cayenne and extract of boneset weed to settle the stomach. The rhubarb was cut for pies as well as medicines to cure everything from cholera to constipation.

Snow Farm was the essence of western Massachusetts. Isolated, it had to succeed as a little world of its own or perish. The abandoned cellar holes scattered throughout its woods remain today as haunting testimony to the men who couldn't control the land and were forced to push on, trying for survival somewhere more gentle and forgiving.

There is no doubt that living was easier along the flat shores of the Chesapeake where dinner hid in the seaweed or lurked beside a piling.

For man eats the food around him. Only the most sophisticated civilizations have ventured beyond their borders for delicacies.

It was thus a natural evolvement for the southern Marylander to develop a wide variety of seafood dishes while the New Englander ate fowl and beef and pork with a little mountain trout thrown in.

Southern Maryland's flat fields, bordered with streams and creeks poking along to the Bay remain today a natural refueling stop for the ducks and geese on their way South. And these remain favorite foods today.

Rabbit, squirrel and deer were everywhere. Even when my mother was growing up, rabbit was a frequent sight on the table. The last fifty years have seen the disappearance of game, which probably accounts for the relatively small number of recipes. They fell into disuse and were forgotten.

One of the most interesting contrasts is in baking. Both used Indian meal, as cornmeal was then called, extensively. But New England developed the drier types, such as johnny cake, while the south liked the softer fork breads such as spoonbread and our cornbread. As a rule, Snow cakes and breads are heartier and heavier than any from the Mosses. And whoever heard of New England grits?

Our southern Maryland taste for butter and fat was greater than that of the Snows. We cooked our vegetables in water seasoned with meat fat, while the Snows just cooked in water and put some butter on to serve.

One great difference is in the use of spirits. The Marylander did and the New Englander didn't. This habit does not seem to be true of the abstaining Snows alone, but of the area, for we were still making our own wine when I was growing up, and cooking with wine, brandy and bourbon goes back into the 18th century.

There is another intriguing difference: the greater use of herbs and spices in southern Maryland. This cannot be attributed to the Puritan ethic or to availability. Perhaps it developed because the New England battle with nature was just that much harder, leaving no time to cultivate herbs for flavor? Certainly they were used medicinally and spices were essential for preserving and pickling, so the awareness of them existed.

I have enjoyed gathering this family harvest which is proof that good American cooking did and does exist, dependent not on sauces and the masking of flavors, but on simple foods prepared in a relatively simple manner.

I hope you will enjoy sharing our family traditions.

SOUPS

ONION SOUP

Best done ahead, cooled and reheated, as the flavors blend in deliciously.

For 4 people.

> 3 *cups chicken stock*
> 2 *tablespoons butter*
> 1 *clove minced garlic*
> 2 *cups chopped onions*
> ¼ *cup wine*
> *thick chunks of buttered bread*
> *Parmesan cheese*

If you do not have a rich, homemade chicken stock, page 25, dissolve 4 cubes of chicken bouillon in 3½ cups of water, add chopped parsley, celery and tops, a bit of basil, pepper to taste, and simmer slowly until well flavored. Strain.

Melt butter in a heavy saucepan. Mince garlic and sauté lightly. Add chopped onions and cook until just transparent. Add stock and wine, simmering slowly until done, about 20 minutes.

Cool soup if possible. Upon reheating or before serving, butter bread and toast it. Pour the soup over the toast, sprinkle with Parmesan cheese. Serve hot.

BLACK-EYED PEA SOUP

This was our traditional New Year's Day dish, guaranteed to bring good luck in the coming year. When I was living in New York back in the '60's, I'd cooked up a batch as usual one New Year's and left it on the stove. When the maid came in, I told her to help herself, putting the rest in the icebox. After a bit, she came trotting down the hall to find me, saying: "My Lord, Miz Snow, I didn't know you ate soul food!"

Mother always served the soup with waffles, but I rather like cornbread or garlic bread with it. A great luncheon or supper for a bunch of jaded appetites. Freezes well, also.

For 8 to 10 people.

> 1 *pound of black-eyed peas*
> *water*
> *hambone with meat bits (or ½ pound lean salt pork)*
> *celery and tops*
> 2 *carrots*
> 2 *onions*
> 10 *peppercorns*
> *salt to taste*

Soak peas overnight in clear water. Drain.

Put hambone into 3 quarts of water and simmer about 45 minutes or until broth is flavorful.

Add several stalks of chopped celery, chopped tops, carrots, a couple of quartered onions, peppercorns and peas. Simmer very slowly for about 3 hours, checking occasionally to be sure water hasn't boiled down. Correct seasoning. Most hams are pretty salty, but you may need a dash.

Dip out any vegetables that are whole and the bone. Serve without straining.

SPLIT PEA SOUP

Follow recipe for black-eyed peas, substituting 1 pound of dried split peas. The split peas will cook down to a rich thick soup.

DRIED BEAN SOUP

Follow recipe for black-eyed peas, substituting 1 pound of dried beans. Cook for the length of time recommended on package, usually from 1½ to 2 hours. Serve without mashing or sieving.

LENTIL SOUP

Follow the recipe for black-eyed peas, substituting 1 pound of dried lentils. Cook 1½ hours. Serve without mashing or sieving.

CORN CHOWDER

All you need for a hearty lunch or supper, served with crackers or crunchy bread. It's a real treat for guests.

For 4 people.

> ½ *cup lean salt pork, bacon or a combination*
> 1 *chopped medium onion*
> 1 *teaspoon chopped parsley*
> 1 *tablespoon chopped green pepper*
> 4 *cubed potatoes*
> 1½ *cups boiling water*
> 2 *cups whole kernel corn, canned or fresh*
> 2 *cups milk*
> *salt and pepper to taste*

Chop pork or bacon into small pieces and cook slowly in a heavy, deep skillet. Meanwhile, chop onion, parsley, green pepper and cube potatoes.

When pork is cooked, remove from the skillet and reserve. Cook the onions in the fat until transparent. Add the parsley, green pepper, potatoes and boiling water. Add cooked meat. Simmer slowly until potatoes are tender, about ½ hour.

Add canned corn and milk, heat to the boiling point. (If fresh corn is used, allow it to cook about 5 minutes in the potato mixture before adding the milk.) Season to taste.

CLAM CHOWDER

Best made with fresh clams, but delicious even with canned. Whether you've wandered down to the water at low tide, wiggled your toes in the sand and dug a bucketful or simply picked up some from your friendly fishmarket, be sure you allow plenty of time to clean them. Nothing's worse than a sandy clam!

Dump them in a bucket of fresh water, add about ½ cup of cornmeal or flour and let them sit and spit for hours, preferably overnight. Then rinse them and scrub with a rough brush.

Put about 4 inches of water in a kettle, add the clams, cover tightly and steam for 5 to 10 minutes until they open. Don't overcook, as they'll get tough. Of course, you *can* eat them right then, dipping them into the broth and melted butter. But save enough to make this chowder, and save all the broth. It's great to drink and has even cured a hangover.

For 4 people.

> *5 slices bacon*
> *½ cup chopped onion*
> *2 tablespoons chopped green pepper*
> *2 cups cubed potatoes*
> *2 cups water and clam juice—try for ½ and ½*
> *1 to 2 cups chopped clams*
> *1 cup cream*
> *1 cup milk*
> *salt and pepper to taste*

Using a heavy saucepan, cut bacon up and fry until brown and beginning to crisp. Add chopped onions and green pepper and sauté until onions are just transparent. Add cubed potatoes and toss around in the fat until they are well coated. Add water and clam juice, cover and simmer until potatoes are just tender, about 30 minutes.

Add chopped clams, milk and cream and bring just to the boil so clams are hot. Season with salt and pepper to taste. Serve at once.

SNOW'S FISH CHOWDER

Some meats and fish were smoked or salted, some vegetables laid down in the cold cellars, but always there were the foods that demanded ice. The milk had to be chilled, the butter cooled, the fresh fish kept. The huge iceboxes were unceasing in their demand for replenishment, and, as the sun warmed the earth, any use of cold rooms ceased.

A century ago when my grandfather was a boy, they were often able to chop their own ice from the frozen shallows of Mosse Pond, storing it in icehouses semi-buried in the earth. But as Maryland winters warmed over the years, most ice was shipped down the Bay by boat from the north and so had to be purchased.

At Snow Farm, however, they continued to make ice until well into this century, amply supplying the iceboxes at the house as well as the huge vats where the milk was chilled before being shipped, and selling the neighboring farmers all they needed.

The Pond was their ice machine. Sparkling in the summer sun, clear and cold as iced tea, with the trout breaking for flies silently interrupting its placidity, it was a swimming heaven in the heat and a skating rink in the winter.

As soon as it froze at least 16 inches deep, the ice making began. Grids about 18 inches square were marked out on the surface with a big icesaw which cut some 6 inches deep. Then a few cakes were cut further with another saw until they floated free.

One of the great drayhorses was hitched with a long cable on a pulley to several cakes by special tongs. Slowly he pulled the ice ashore, up a ramp to the door of the icehouse where it was stacked, layered with sawdust.

There it stayed in icy perfection until the Pond once again froze deep. Thus, when the fishmonger came by wagon from Boston with his wares in barrels of ice, or some trout or perch were hooked in the stream, there was no problem in keeping them iced until ready for use.

With whitefish from the fishmonger, here is how they made a chowder.

For 6 people.

> *2 cups whitefish*
> *¼ pound lean salt pork*
> *2 medium onions, sliced*
> *6 small potatoes, sliced*
> *water*
> *6 soda crackers*
> *salt and pepper to taste*
> *1 quart milk*

Bone and cut fish into small pieces. Cut rind off pork and slice quite thin. Put pork into a deep, heavy skillet or pot and fry until brown and crisp, adding the sliced onions when you turn the pork, so that they can become golden and transparent.

Pare and slice potatoes thin. When pork and onions are browned, layer the potatoes over them. Add the cut up fish. Add just enough water to cover. Cover pot and simmer for ½ hour.

Pound the crackers into meal and pour into pot. Taste for seasoning, adding salt if needed and pepper to taste. Add milk and bring to the boil, but do not let it boil. Serve hot.

OYSTER STEW

This comes under the fast food department, and makes the most wonderfully satisfying lunch or supper. Follow it with a cottage pudding and custard.

For 2 people.

    8 ounces oysters (½ pint or about 12)
    1½ tablespoons butter
    1 tablespoon chopped onion
    ¾ cup cream
    1½ cups milk
    oyster liquor
    1 tablespoon finely chopped parsley
    salt and pepper to taste

Drain oysters, reserving liquor. Melt butter in a deep, heavy skillet and sauté onions until transparent but not brown.

Heat milk, cream and liquor together, but do not scald.

Drop the oysters into the onions and let cook just a minute, until the edges begin to curl.

Pour oysters and onions with fat into the hot milk, add the finely chopped parsley, salt and pepper to taste, and heat until the oysters float. Serve at once.

If you must hold the stew for a bit, heat the milk in the top of a double boiler and proceed with recipe.

SCALLOP STEW

A delectable treat, this is made rather like an oyster stew. Serve it with a green vegetable and a loaf of homemade bread.

For 3 people.

    2 tablespoons minced onions
    3 tablespoons butter
    1 pound scallops
    1 cup milk
    2 cups cream
    salt and pepper to taste
    several sprigs chopped parsley

Mince onion well. Melt 2 tablespoons of the butter in a deep, heavy pot and sauté the onions until they turn transparent. Add the scallops and just mix around in the pot for a couple of minutes to coat them.

Meanwhile, mix the milk and cream and have hot. Pour into the scallop pot, add the remaining butter and salt and pepper to taste, let heat through.

Sprinkle with the chopped parsley and serve at once.

CRAB SOUP

If you're having steamed or fried hard crabs, this is the ideal follow-up, as you can use the legs, claws and leftover meat. Or steam a few just for this.

For 4 to 6 people.

> 3 *slices of bacon*
> ½ *green pepper, finely chopped*
> 3 *stalks celery, finely chopped*
> 1 *medium onion, finely chopped*
> 2 *tablespoons chopped parsley*
> 2 *cups tomatoes*
> 2 *cups water*
> *salt and pepper to taste*
> *crab claws and legs*
> 1 *pound regular crab*

Cut bacon into small pieces and fry until crisp. Remove from fat and reserve. Sauté the vegetables in the fat for 4 to 5 minutes. add tomatoes, water, salt and pepper, and cook for ½ hour at a low simmer. If you have crab legs and claws, add with the tomatoes.

Pick over crab carefully.

Dip out the legs and claws, add the crab and simmer for 8 more minutes.

Sprinkle bacon over the soup and serve.

CHICKEN STOCK OR SOUP

This is an indispensable stock which I make and freeze for futures. It makes an unbeatable chicken vegetable soup too. Save up your leftover roast or broiled chicken carcasses or start with one, if you must. Or start with the neck, wings and giblets. If meat is sparse, add a bouillon cube or two.

FOR STOCK
chicken carcass, and any pieces
4 cups water
1 cut up onion
4 sprigs of parsley
1 teaspoon salt
6 peppercorns
several celery stalks and tops
3 to 4 crumbled basil leaves
½ teaspoon sugar

Combine all ingredients but the sugar in a kettle, cover and simmer until the meat falls off the bones. Strain. Add the sugar. Correct seasoning.

FOR SOUP
4 cups stock
2 quartered potatoes
2 sliced carrots
4 cut up stalks celery
2 cups tomatoes

Combine all ingredients in a kettle, cover and simmer slowly until vegetables are done. Correct seasoning.

TURKEY SOUP

Proceed as above to make the stock, substituting pieces of turkey carcass, doubling ingredients. Double amount of vegetables.

TOMATO SOUP

Cousin Mattie Guilford was a spinster who lived at Snow Farm for many years, until one day she upped and went to California, never to return. This is her tomato soup "mixture" as the old records read.

Makes about 8 quarts.

> ½ *bushel ripe tomatoes*
> 2 *quarts water*
> 12 *tablespoons cornstarch dissolved in water*
> 1 *cup butter*
> 8 *sliced onions*
> *salt and pepper to taste*
> 1 *cup sugar*

Stem tomatoes and cut into small pieces without skinning. Bring water to a boil and boil tomatoes 10 minutes. Dissolve cornstarch in a little bit of water and add. Stir well.

Melt butter and fry the sliced onions in it until golden brown. Add to the tomatoes, season with salt and pepper to taste, simmer for 15 minutes. Strain.

Return to the stove, add the sugar and simmer again for a few minutes until blended well. Correct seasonings.

Seal in hot sterilized jars.

SEAFOOD AND FISH

THAT CRAZY CRAB

The Lord must have made it taste so good to make up for its peculiar appearance. And man has braved its looks for its flavor for millennia. The early Romans immortalized the crab in mosaics uncovered in Britain. Apicius, the famed 3rd century gourmet, loved crab served whole, boiled or whatever. His recipe for crab sausage was boiled crab mixed with spikenard, garum, pepper and eggs, then placed on a stove or gridiron. He also flavored it with a seasoning sauce of pepper, cumin, rue mixed with garum, honey, oil and vinegar.

I've found nothing like these in our records, but there's no doubt that the crab to a southern Marylander ranks with mother, God and country.

As a child, half the fun was catching them, sitting in the sun with a piece of rotten eel dangling at the end of a line. All it took was a lot of patience and a sure hand, while it left a bit of time just for dreaming. Soft crabs were an easy catch. Just a sharp eye to spot them hidden in the seaweed along the shore, a fast dip with the net and another one joined the batch in the peachbasket.

The crab is misunderstood in most places. There are three kinds of meat from the hard crab. Backfin, which is usually called lump, is the pure white meat from the body of the crab. It is the choice meat and must be used for salads, cocktail and imperial crab.

Regular or special is the meat from the ribbed part of the crab mixed with bits of backfin. Claw is obviously from the claws. Regular and claw are slightly sweeter than backfin and should be used in crab cakes, cutlets and soup. Regular can be used in casseroles also, and, since the price of backfin is rather breathtaking, it usually is.

Unfortunately, outside of Maryland, most markets sell nothing but backfin. Make friends with your seafood man and get him to order you regular or claw. You may have to educate him on the difference. To my taste, canned crab is a waste of money, but it can be tossed into a casserole to fill out the quantity if you run short of the fresh.

The soft crab is eaten whole, legs, claws and all. It just needs cleaning and, I understand, courage for the uninitiated.

STEAMED HARD CRABS

First, go catch a mess of them. Toss back all the females and undersized ones, and, please, don't keep more than you can use. (Females have a broad apron with a tiny spike; males have a sharply spiked apron.) Dump them in a bucket of seawater as you catch them—they must be kept alive until they're cooked.

Back at the ranch, fill a big kettle about ⅓ to ½ full with water, 2 cups of vinegar, a bottle of stale beer if you have it, about ½ cup of salt, plenty of celery salt, about ¼ to ½ cup each of red and black pepper and bring to a boil. Dump the crabs in, cover immediately and cook about 20 minutes. They'll turn red and the aprons will begin to loosen when they're done.

Now, hop into some jeans or a bathing suit, spread out some newspapers, set out a loaf of hearty bread and a crock of butter, open a beer, stack up plenty of napkins and have a pail of handwashing water handy. You're ready for a fast trip to heaven.

If you can, con one and all into picking a crab for the pot, so you'll have meat for another feast all ready.

FRIED HARD CRABS

I call this a seven-petticoat dish, because it's a messy feast. Seven petticoats were the equivalent of blue jeans when my grandmother was a girl. When she was laced and dressed, she wore thirteen! And she never ceased to deplore the fact that her waist laced only to 20 inches while her sister's got down to 17. Whatever, there's no doubt that when great-grandmother served fried hard crabs, no one was laced and dressed.

Spread some newspapers on a table, have a cold pitcher of beer, a tossed salad, some crusty bread and plenty of paper towels handy with fingerbowls or a couple of pails of water.

Allow 3 to 6 crabs per person.

Steam crabs, see page 28, and clean, removing claws and legs which may be saved for soup.

Heat hot bacon fat (or butter) in heavy skillet, having about ½″ of fat. Fry the crab bodies about 3 minutes per side. Serve at once.

CRAB CAKES

Most famous and, probably, most beloved of all crab dishes, these are also nice and easy. Serve hot or cold, as an entree or a picnic sandwich. For dinner, slaw, glazed carrots, peas and dumplings or asparagus with cornbread and potatoes make a heavenly meal. Tartar sauce is optional.

Figure on 10 to 12 cakes per pound of crabmeat.

> *1 pound regular, special or claw crab*
> *2 slices dry white bread, preferably 2 days old*
> *⅛ teaspoon red pepper*
> *1 tablespoon finely minced green pepper*
> *1 tablespoon finely chopped parsley*
> *1 teaspoon dry mustard*
> *¼ teaspoon salt*
> *2 eggs, slightly beaten*
> *up to ⅓ cup milk*
> *black pepper to taste*
> *½ stick butter, melted*

Pick crab. Crumble bread quite small. Add red pepper, green

pepper, parsley, mustard and salt. Put into slightly beaten eggs to which 2 tablespoons of milk have been added. Add crab, mixing lightly with a two-pronged fork to keep it light. Add a couple more tablespoons of milk, continuing to add only until mixture has a consistency that will let you form cakes. Taste for seasonings and add black pepper if desired. Mix in melted butter lightly.

Shape into cakes ½ inch thick and 2 to 3 inches in diameter. Cook on a slightly greased griddle over high heat, turning once, about 10 minutes. When brown, they are done.

If you plan to freeze them, cook until a pale gold only, about 5 minutes. Wrap in foil. They may then be sautéed for 6 to 8 minutes on top of the stove or placed in the foil for 20 minutes in a preheated moderate (350°) oven.

CRAB CUTLETS

This is a slightly richer version of the crab cake and suitable for home meals only.

For 4 to 6 people.

Proceed exactly as in the recipe for crab cakes, substituting the following thick white sauce for the breadcrumbs.

> 3 *tablespoons butter*
> 3 *tablespoons flour*
> 1 *cup milk*
> ¼ *tablespoon salt*
> *dash of red pepper*

Melt butter and slowly stir in flour, cooking and stirring constantly for 3 to 4 minutes. Warm milk and add slowly, continuing to stir constantly until sauce is thick and at the simmer point. Add seasonings and proceed with remainder of crab cake recipe.

IMPERIAL CRAB

Justly named, it is rich, elegant to look at and, unfortunately, expensive. Unless money is no object, save it for a foursome dinner.

You'll need 4 crab or clam shells or ramekins of some sort. Keep your menu rather bland, as the flavor of the crab is too delicate to do battle with highly seasoned foods. Gnocchi à la Lorraine (p. 113), tomato aspic (p. 107), asparagus and hot rolls are perfect friends.

For 4 people.

> 1 *pound backfin (lump) crab*
> ½ *teaspoon salt*
> ¼ *teaspoon black pepper*
> *dash red pepper*
> 1 *tablespoon finely minced green pepper*
> ½ *tablespoon finely chopped parsley*
> ½ *cup mayonnaise*
> 2 *teaspoons dry mustard*
> *additional mayonnaise*
> *sliced pimientos*

Preheat oven to 325°.

Pick crab carefully, being cautious so you do not break up the lumps. Mix all other ingredients except the additional mayonnaise and pimiento together. Using a two-pronged fork, carefully toss the crab into the mayonnaise mixture. Butter shells and place crab in each one, heaping it up in the center. Put a small teaspoon of mayonnaise on top of each. Lay one or two thin slices of pimiento across the top.

Bake in a moderate (325°) oven until brown, approximately 25 minutes. Serve at once.

CRAB SALAD

My mother always used to say this was the only way to serve backfin, as the flavor was too good to adulterate with any other ingredients. For a delectable luncheon or supper, serve with hot bread, a chilled white wine and follow with a lemon caketop pudding (p. 168).

For 3 people.

1 *pound backfin (lump) crab*	*sliced cucumbers*
1 *teaspoon lemon juice*	*mayonnaise*
crisp lettuce	*capers (optional)*
sliced green pepper rings	

Pick crab carefully, being cautious not to break up lumps. Squeeze lemon juice over it. Make a bed of lettuce and place crab on it. Put green pepper ring on top and sliced cucumbers around the edge. Serve mayonnaise in a separate sauceboat. Serve capers separately if used.

CRAB CASSEROLE À LA LORRAINE

An ambrosial dish, brought to perfection by my mother, and a guarantee of a gourmet reputation on the spot. Serve with tomato aspic (p. 107), baked grits (p. 112) or gnocchi (p. 113), raised biscuits and a chilled white wine. Note that this dish can be made ahead.

For 6 to 8 people.

THE CRAB
1 *pound backfin or regular crab*
1 *cup shrimp or lobster (optional)*
2 *slices dry white bread*
2 *tablespoons milk*
2 *tablespoons melted butter*

THE SAUCE

6 tablespoons melted butter
6 tablespoons flour
1¾ cups milk
¼ cup sherry or dry vermouth
1 teaspoon salt
1 teaspoon dry mustard
1 teaspoon Worcestershire sauce
1/16 teaspoon red pepper
dash of Tabasco
dash of black pepper
2 lightly beaten eggs
½ cup mushrooms (optional)

THE TOPPING

½ cup fine breadcrumbs
3 tablespoons butter

Preheat oven to 325°.

Pick over crab carefully, being cautious not to break it up. If using large shrimp, cut them up. Crumble bread in fine crumbs, add the milk to breadcrumbs and soak for several hours. Fork lightly into the crab, add melted butter and mix lightly. Set aside for a few minutes while you prepare sauce.

Using the top of a double boiler, melt the butter, then add the flour slowly, stirring constantly over low heat for about 3 to 4 minutes until cooked. Slowly add the milk, continuing to stir constantly. Add spirits and all seasonings and bring just to the boil. You may do this over boiling water rather than direct heat, as it precludes any chance of scorching.

Beat eggs lightly, then spoon some of the white sauce into them, whipping constantly. Continue to combine sauce with the eggs, whipping as you do until all the sauce is in and you have a foamy look.

Return the sauce to the double boiler, put back over lightly boiling water and cook until you have a custard consistency, about 1 minute. Correct seasoning: sauce should be hot, and you may wish to increase the Tabasco and mustard.

Butter a casserole. Put in a layer of the sauce, then a layer of the crab, until all is used up, ending with sauce on top. Sprinkle the topping of breadcrumbs over it, dot with butter. You may refrigerate it at this point and bake later.

Bake in a moderate (325°) oven until brown and bubbly, about 25 minutes. Do not overcook or sauce will become watery. Serve at once.

BAKED CRAB

A simple, simply delicious entree for a dinner party with baked onions or tomatoes, a gnocchi, salad and hot rolls. A dry white wine should be served.

For 6 to 8.

> 2 pounds backfin or regular crab
> 2 slices dry white bread
> ½ cup milk
> 1 tablespoon sherry
> ¼ teaspoon Tabasco
> 1 teaspoon dry mustard
> dash cayenne
> 2 to 3 tablespoons finely chopped green pepper
> 1 tablespoon finely chopped parsley
> 4 tablespoons softened butter
> 2 lightly beaten eggs

Preheat oven to 350°.

Pick crab carefully trying not to break up the flakes. Crumble the bread quite fine and soak in milk, preferably overnight.

Combine all the remaining ingredients except the eggs and toss lightly. Stir into the eggs. Fold, using a two-pronged fork, quite lightly into the bread. Then, just as lightly, fold the crab into the mixture.

Grease a casserole and spoon crab into it. You may refrigerate at this point and bake later. You may also use individual shells or ramekins, decreasing the baking time by 5 minutes. Bake the casserole in a moderate (350°) oven for 25 minutes until hot and bubbly.

DEVILED CRAB

This is a hot, drier crab dish than the crab cake. It was always made in the shells from the steamed crabs. If you don't have any crab shells, they can be bought. Ramekins don't really work as well.

For 4 deviled crabs—1 apiece.

> 1 *pound regular or special crab*
> 3 *slices dry white bread, preferably 2 days old*
> ½ *teaspoon red pepper*
> 1 *tablespoon finely chopped parsley*
> 1 *teaspoon dry mustard*
> ⅛ *teaspoon salt*
> 2 *eggs, slightly beaten*
> *up to* ⅓ *cup milk*
> *several squirts of Tabasco*
> *black pepper to taste*
> ½ *stick butter, melted*

Preheat oven to 325°.

Have crab shells scrubbed and buttered. Pick crab. Crumble bread quite small. Add red pepper, parsley, mustard and salt. Put into slightly beaten eggs to which 2 tablespoons of milk have been added. Add several squirts of Tabasco. Add crab, mixing lightly with two-pronged fork to keep it light. Add a couple more tablespoons of milk, continuing just until mixture has consistency that holds together. Taste for seasonings. Remember, it should be hot, but let it sit on your tongue a moment, swallow and wait a minute or two for the heat to come through before you add any more of anything. Add black pepper if needed, and the melted butter.

Place crab shells on cookie sheet, pile with the crab mixture and bake in the moderate (325°) oven until browned, about 25 minutes. Do not overcook as they will dry out.

Serve hot or cold.

CRAB BALLS

These are so good they probably should be outlawed. They're guaranteed to make a cocktail party work. (They start out like crab cakes, but wind up different.)

Makes 300 balls—for 50 to 60 people.

> *4 pounds regular or special crab*
> *1½ slices dry white bread, preferably 2 days old*
> *½ teaspoon red pepper*
> *4 tablespoons finely minced green pepper*
> *4 tablespoons finely chopped parsley*
> *4 teaspoons dry mustard*
> *½ teaspoon salt*
> *8 eggs, slightly beaten*
> *up to 1⅓ cups milk*
> *black pepper to taste*
> *4 sticks butter, melted*

Do this first part in the morning. Pick crab. Crumble bread quite small. Add red pepper, green pepper, parsley, mustard and salt. Put into slightly beaten eggs to which ½ cup of milk has been added. Add crab, mixing lightly with a two-pronged fork to keep it light. Add ½ cup more milk, continuing to add only until mixture has a consistency that will let you form balls. Taste for seasonings and add black pepper if desired. Mix in melted butter lightly.

Heat vegetable fat in a deep-fat fryer—use a deep 3- or 4-quart kettle with enough fat to come up half way. Heat to 365°. (If you don't have a deep-fry thermometer, test with a 1″ bread cube: throw it into the hot fat, and if it browns in one minute, the temperature's right.)

Place balls in a wire basket, lower into fat and fry until slightly golden. Do this in batches until all are done, then refrigerate until ready to serve. These may also be frozen.

Preheat broiler to 400°. Place crab balls on broiler sheet or in flat pan. Set on middle rack and run under the heat until brown— just a minute. Serve with toothpicks while hot.

SHERRIED CRAB

Absolutely yummy cocktail party dish. Serve in a chafing dish and let your guests just dip it out with melba toast. I eat any leftovers with a fork.

For 16 to 20 people.

> 2 *pounds regular crab*
> 1¾ *pounds shrimp (optional)*
>
> THE SAUCE
> ½ *cup butter*
> 8 *tablespoons flour*
> 1 *scant teaspoon salt*
> 13-*ounce can evaporated milk*
> 1 *cup dry sherry*
> 1 *teaspoon Worcestershire sauce*
> *pepper to taste*

Pick crab carefully without breaking up. Cut up shrimp small. Set aside.

Make the sauce by melting the butter in top of a double boiler, then adding the flour and salt, cooking and stirring constantly for a few minutes. Remove from heat and place over boiling water. Gradually add the milk, stirring constantly. Add the sherry a little at a time, being careful not to get sauce too thin. Add Worcestershire sauce. Sauce will be very thick and rich. Add pepper.

Carefully, when sauce is hot, add crab and shrimp. Try not

to break up the crab flakes as you mix it in. Let it all heat, then remove to chafing dish.

FRIED SOFT CRABS

I have the distinct feeling that if my mother were asked to prepare a picnic menu for heaven, she'd order soft crab sandwiches and beer! And I'd be right beside her.

If you're serving for dinner, they go beautifully with baked grits, potatoes, tomatoes in any form, succotash, what have you. Allow 2 apiece unless they are very small.

But only live soft crabs, if you haven't netted your own. Even though they're packed in ice, the claws and legs should move a bit. To clean them, take a very sharp knife, cut off the face just back of the eyes. Remove the apron, the spongy parts (dead men's fingers), gills, stomach and intestines under the points of the shell and from the center of the body.

Rinse in cold water, drain and pat dry.

Salt and pepper them well, then roll lightly in flour.

Melt enough butter or margarine in a heavy skillet to give you about ⅛" of fat, getting it hot but not smoking. Fry the crabs until brown on one side, then turn. The shells will become red, the claws and legs fairly crisp.

After they have browned, cover and allow to cook at the lowest possible temperature about 15 minutes until tender and succulent.

Serve at once.

THE ROYAL OYSTER

The man seated before a mess of oysters becomes a king, and for millennia, man has been crowning himself. Along the shores of the Mediterranean, some huge piles of shells thousands of years old remain mute leftovers of ancient banquets. These early oyster-men never developed the wit to toss the shells back into the sea as nurturing ground for other creatures, nor did they learn to cultivate them until Roman times.

Along the shores of the Chesapeake, the American Indian pried open the rough shells for his feasts, leaving strata after strata of them in the clay banks of Calvert County. He introduced the first settlers to the bounty of the waters, thereby producing the complaint by fourscore of the Jamestown settlers in 1607 that they "fed upon nothing but oysters eight weeks apace."

The colonists not only learned to eat the oyster but eventually to mix the shells into the mortar of their homes and to crush them for roads. By the middle of the 19th century, the oyster had become such a sought-after delicacy that the beds were being stripped without thought of seeding. The oyster was threatened with extinction. Virginia and Maryland oystermen fought as bit-terly over the diminishing beds as ever their ancestors had over Yorktown. Stringent legislation has saved the beds and keeps an uneasy truce among the men.

The old oyster boats have almost disappeared from the Bay. I can remember when their sails were as familiar as the gulls and the dock was full of their funny, sway-backed hulls, smelly and dirty after days at sea. If there had been a good haul, they rode low along the gunn'ls, while the reddened leather of the men's faces showed a rare crack of pleasure.

Oysters are synonymous with Christmas Eve to me. Around midnight when the awesome silence began to settle over the town, we would gather in my grandfather's kitchen with a bushel of oysters still wet from the Bay. It was a noisy feast as everyone vied for the next oyster. Walt, my most enterprising younger brother, became an expert shucker in self-defense, discovering at thirteen that the only way to get enough was to do it himself, thus guaran-teeing 2 for every 1 dispensed.

At that point, all anyone needed was a drop of lemon juice, although some resorted to homemade chili sauce. And today, that is still a choice way to eat the Royal Oyster.

OYSTER SCALLOP

Any self-respecting oyster would be proud to be in this delicacy. You may prepare it ahead, stick it in the refrigerator until time to bake. Serve with a colorful vegetable such as tomatoes or squashes, potatoes or rice, hot rolls and a white wine.

Prepare in individual casseroles or 1 flat baking dish.

For 4 people.

> 1 *pint oysters*
> 2 *tablespoons lemon juice*
> ½ *cup of butter*
> 3 *slices of white bread, crumbed*
> 1 *tablespoon grated onion*
> *salt and pepper to taste*
> *grating of nutmeg*

Preheat oven to 350°.

Drain oysters. Tear them into two or three pieces. Pour the lemon juice over them and let stand.

Melt ⅓ of a cup of the butter, letting the remainder soften. Break the bread into small crumbs, but not powder. Add the melted butter and grated onion to them.

Grease casserole and layer the bread into it, layer some oysters over the bread, dot with softened butter, sprinkle with salt and pepper. Repeat the layers. Cover the last layer with breadcrumbs completely, dot with the remaining butter and grate nutmeg over the top.

Bake in the moderate (350°) oven about 20 minutes until brown and crisp on top. Oysters will puff and their edges will ruffle when they are done.

Serve at once.

OYSTER PIE

A mighty good way to eat oysters. Best done in individual pies, as one large one is a bit difficult to serve. Baked grits or rice, asparagus and an aspic make nice additions to the menu.

For 4 people.

> *piecrust (p. 177)*
> *4 tablespoons butter*
> *5 tablespoons chopped onion*
> *5 tablespoons chopped celery*
> *2 tablespoons minced parsley*
> *4 tablespoons flour*
> *1 cup oyster liquor*
> *2 cups light cream*
> *½ to ¾ teaspoons mace*
> *salt and pepper to taste*
> *1½ pints oysters*

Preheat oven to 450°.

Prepare piecrust and line 4 individual pie pans. Cut top crusts to fit and place on a cookie sheet. You will have to bake the bottom crusts until done, about 12–15 minutes, and the top crusts until almost done. The filling is put into cooked crusts, then covered with the top crusts and then the pies run under the broiler just to brown the top crust, about 3 to 4 minutes.

Melt butter in the top of a heavy double boiler. Add chopped onion, celery and parsley, and over direct heat, sauté until the onions are transparent and the celery softened. Gradually stir in flour and continue to stir and cook for 3 to 4 minutes. Slowly pour in oyster liquor and cream, stirring constantly and cooking until you have a smooth, rich sauce. It will be thick. Add mace and salt and pepper to taste.

Add oysters and allow to cook in the sauce over slowly simmering water for about 5 minutes.

Pour into the baked crusts, cover with the top crusts, run under the broiler at 350° and brown. Serve at once.

FRIED OYSTERS

Fried oysters are so elementary that I hesitated to include them, but realizing that so many poor, benighted oysters get incarcerated in thick batters that disguise their delicacy, I hereby do.

Allow 4 to 5 oysters per person, depending on size.

> *drained oysters*
> 1 *beaten egg*
> 1 *tablespoon water*
> *crackermeal seasoned with salt and pepper*
> *butter*

Drain oysters and pat dry. Beat egg and combine with water. Have meal well seasoned. Melt enough butter in a heavy skillet to more than coat it heavily—it should be visible, not just greased as for griddle cakes—and have it hot but not sizzling.

Dip oysters in the egg, then the crackermeal and repeat if necessary. They should be coated all over. Fry them in the fat, turning once, about 3 to 5 minutes, until browned.

Serve at once with catchup.

STEAMED SHRIMP

For cocktails, salads or any dishes requiring cooked shrimp, this method will give you flavorful, tender ones.

> *fresh shrimp*
> *water to cover*
> ½ *cup vinegar*
> *several celery tops*
> *several dashes of red pepper*
> ½ *to 1 teaspoon salt*

Be sure shrimp are nice and fresh. Estimate the amount of water needed just to cover them in a kettle. Add all other ingredients and bring water to a boil, boiling 5 minutes.

Add shrimp, cooking small ones about 3 minutes and large ones about 5 to 6. They will turn red and curl when done.

Shell, remove heads and tails, devein if they need it. If you are planning to stuff them, leave the tails on.

SHRIMP DE JONGE

An exceptional do-ahead entree, good with baked onions, escalloped potatoes, a tossed salad and a dry white wine.

For 8 people.

> 2 pounds steamed shrimp (p. 42)
> 1 cup butter
> 4–5 sliced cloves of garlic
> ¼ teaspoon each: tarragon, minced parsley, minced shallots, minced onions
> dash each: nutmeg, mace, thyme
> 2 teaspoons salt
> ¼ teaspoon pepper
> ½ cup consommé or dry sherry
> 1 cup fine breadcrumbs

Preheat oven to 400°.

Place cooked shrimp in casserole or 8 individual casseroles. Melt butter in a heavy skillet and sauté the garlic until the butter browns, then remove it. Do not let butter burn. Add the herbs, seasonings and consommé or sherry. Heat to the simmer.

Pour ¼ of the butter mixture into the breadcrumbs and toss lightly. Pour the remainder of the butter mixture over the shrimp. Top the shrimp with buttered breadcrumbs. Bake in hot (400°) oven for 15 minutes.

If prepared ahead and refrigerated, preheat oven to 350° and bake for 20 minutes or until hot through.

FRIED SHRIMP

Decapitate, shell and devein, leaving the tails on. They may be picked up and eaten, holding them by the tails.

Allow 4 or 5 shrimp per person.

> 1 *beaten egg*
> *little water or milk*
> *seasoned breadcrumbs*
> *butter*

Dry shrimp. Add a bit of milk or water to the beaten egg, about 1 tablespoonful. Dip the shrimp in the egg, then in the seasoned breadcrumbs. Repeat if necessary to coat them well.

Melt enough butter in a heavy skillet so that pan is more than generously coated. Fry the shrimp swiftly in it, about 4 to 5 minutes per side.

Serve at once.

STUFFED BAKED SHRIMP

Shrimp stuffed with crab are on the list of foods I could die for. At one point in my life, I think I ate them twice a week at least. They're rich and should be served with a tossed salad, a simple potato or just hot bread. A rosé or burgundy is preferable with them.

Allow 4 to 5 shrimp per person. You will need jumbo ones.

Steam as for cocktails (p. 42). Slit open.

Make crab stuffing (p. 143).

Stuff each shrimp as full as possible, using toothpicks if necessary to hold them together.

Melt sufficient butter to generously cover the bottom of a flat baking dish or individual casseroles. Lay the shrimp in carefully.

Preheat oven hot (400°) and bake shrimp about 15 minutes or until bubbly and browned slightly. Serve at once.

Bread stuffing (p. 142) may be substituted. It makes a mighty fine meal also.

SHRIMP STROGANOFF

My diminutive and fiery mother once looked at me with slightly veiled disgust and, waving a wooden spoon, informed me that good cooking was nothing but a bit of imagination often bred by necessity.

It took her seafood addiction, imagination and necessity to concoct this unique and delicious entree.

For 4 to 6 people.

> *2 pounds steamed shrimp (p. 42)*
> *6 tablespoons butter*
> *1½ cups sliced mushrooms*
> *2 tablespoons chopped onions*
> *1 clove garlic, minced*
> *3 tablespoons flour*
> *1 cup consommé*
> *1 teaspoon tomato paste*
> *1 teaspoon Worcestershire sauce*
> *1 tablespoon sherry*
> *1 cup sour cream*
> *1 tablespoon chopped parsley*
> *salt and pepper to taste*

Steam shrimp and keep warm. Melt butter in a heavy skillet, add sliced mushrooms and sauté 2 minutes. Add chopped onions and garlic and sauté until tender. Stir in the flour and cook 3 to 4 minutes, stirring constantly. Stir in the consommé and continue to stir while the sauce cooks, until it is smooth and thick. Add tomato paste, Worcestershire sauce and sherry.

Remove from heat and quickly blend in the sour cream and chopped parsley. Season with salt and pepper to taste. Add the warm shrimp.

You may keep this hot in a chafing dish or the top of a double broiler.

Serve over rice or noodles.

SHRIMP CREOLE

If you're forethoughted, as I always say, you can make a batch of this sauce, freeze some of it and have a spectacular dinner for unexpected guests. It also can be made the day before and simply reheated, which makes it ideal for a buffet. Serve with steamed rice, sliced avocado salad and a rosé or burgundy.

For 3 to 4 people.

> 1 *pound steamed shrimp (p. 42)*
> 3 *tablespoons butter*
> ½ *large onion, chopped*
> 1 *clove garlic, minced*
> ½ *green pepper, chopped*
> 3 *tablespoons chopped stuffed olives*
> 1 *chicken bouillon cube*
> 1½ *cups tomatoes*
> ½ *cup tomato paste*
> 1 *teaspoon sugar*
> *cayenne to taste*
> *salt to taste*

Steam shrimp. Melt butter in heavy skillet, add chopped onions, garlic, green pepper and olives. Sauté until onions are transparent. Dissolve the bouillon cube in the tomatoes and add with the tomato paste, sugar, cayenne and salt. Simmer covered about ½ hour or until flavors have blended.

Add shrimp, letting them get hot. Correct seasonings.

CLAM PIE

That friendly little creature, the clam, pops happily into a pie to give you a different taste treat. Serve with vegetables and cornsticks.

Best done as individual pies.

For 4 people.

piecrust (p. 177)
2 cups chopped clams, drained (two 8-ounce cans)
½ cup of the clam liquor
½ cup cream
½–¾ cup seasoned breadcrumbs
salt, pepper and paprika to taste
butter

Preheat oven to 350°.

Prepare piecrust and line pie pans.

Drain clams and reserve liquor. Mix the liquor with the cream. Break your breadcrumbs small but not powdery and season with salt, pepper and paprika to taste. Mix the breadcrumbs and the liquids together, add the clams and mix again lightly. Pour into piecrusts, dot with butter. Cover with a top crust and prick it.

Bake in the moderate (350°) oven for 45 minutes to 1 hour, depending on the size of your pies. They should be brown on top and bubbly inside. Serve at once.

CLAM FRITTERS

Delicately flavored, these fritters are an entree and go well with a green and a yellow vegetable, perhaps some escalloped potatoes and a salad. Allow at least 3 fritters per person.

Makes 12 small fritters.

¾ cup flour
¼ teaspoon salt
1 teaspoon baking powder
1 cup minced clams (8-ounce can)
1 beaten egg
½ chicken bouillon cube
⅓ cup clam juice + 1 tablespoon
⅓ cup milk
dash of pepper
few drops of onion juice

Sift flour, salt and baking powder together. Drain clams and reserve juice. Beat egg. Dissolve bouillon cube in clam juice and combine with egg. Add milk, pepper and onion juice. Stir lightly into the dry ingredients. Mix in clams.

Lightly grease a heavy griddle and have quite hot. Drop a tablespoon of the batter for each fritter on the griddle and fry as you would pancakes, about 2 minutes on each side.

Drain on a paper towel, keep in warm oven until all are done. Serve at once.

CLAM BALLS OR CROQUETTES

The kind of hors d'oeuvres people can't stop eating, these can also be made into croquettes and served as an entree. They must be made 2 days ahead and refrigerated before cooking. They can also be cooked, frozen and simply run into the oven for reheating, then transferred to a chafing dish or passed with toothpicks on a tray.

Makes about 80 balls.

> 1⅓ *cups minced clams (10½-ounce can)*
> 5 *tablespoons butter*
> 6 *tablespoons flour*
> ½ *cup milk*
> ½ *cup clam juice*
> 1 *chicken bouillon cube*
> 5 *squirts Tabasco*
> *small garlic clove, minced*
> *breadcrumbs*
> 1 *beaten egg*
> *additional butter*

Drain clams and reserve juice. Melt butter in a heavy skillet, add flour and cook 2 to 3 minutes, stirring constantly. Remove from heat. Add milk, clam juice, bouillon cube, Tabasco and the minced garlic. Add the clams. Stir well, return to stove and cook until thick, letting it boil for about 2 minutes, stirring constantly. Mixture will be quite thick.

Refrigerate for 2 days.

Make balls by pinching off pieces the size of a hickory nut and shaping into balls. Have breadcrumbs quite fine. Beat egg and dip the balls into it, then into the breadcrumbs. Heat and melt enough butter to cover the bottom of a heavy skillet, having it hot but not sizzling. Fry clam balls until golden brown.

SAUTÉED SCALLOPS

Native to northern waters, the little bay scallop is a creamy treasure. We even love them raw as an hors d'oeuvre . . . just impaled on a toothpick.

For 3 people.

> 1 *pound bay scallops*
> 1 *tablespoon lemon juice*
> 2 *tablespoons minced onion*
> 2 *tablespoons butter*
> *salt and pepper to taste*
> 1 *cup white wine (optional)*

Do not wash scallops, just pat dry. Squeeze lemon juice over them and let stand a few moments. Mince onion well. Heat butter in a heavy skillet and sauté the onions until just transparent. Add the scallops, sprinkle with salt and pepper, add the wine if desired, and sauté gently 3 minutes, turning them for another 3 minutes.

Serve at once. Scallops will toughen if overcooked or held too long.

BAKED FISH FILLETS

The simplest, quickest way to cook small fish. Best if they are freshly caught.

Clean and fillet fish, melt a little butter in a flat baking dish, then lay fish in it. Sprinkle with salt and pepper, pour lemon juice over them and bake in a preheated moderate (325°) oven for 15 to 20 minutes. Serve at once.

BAKED FISH WITH OR WITHOUT STUFFING

The prized Chesapeake Bay fish are the shad and the rockfish. However, you'll find this an admirable way to cook any fish of 3 pounds or over such as bass, red snapper or even blues.

To bake without the stuffing, proceed exactly the same way, but check your cooking time, as you must not overdo it. The fish should be just flaky. Stuffed with crab, it will be ambrosia.

Allow 15 minutes per pound for a stuffed fish in a moderately slow oven (300°), which must be preheated.

Clean and bone and split fish open. Rub inside with a dash of salt and pepper. Anoint with lemon juice. Place flat out in a baking dish.

Stuff with crab or bread stuffing (pp. 143 or 142). Fold top-side over. Rub with a dash of salt and pepper. Swirl a bit of bacon grease, butter or margarine over it. Check your timing and bake in 300° oven. Serve at once.

BROILED FISH

Daddy used to love to row out into the Channel where the Severn meets the Chesapeake, fishing pole in hand, battered hat on head. His favorite companion was my beloved aunt Beppy who didn't talk very much.

The two would spend hours just sitting, rolling with the swells, nodding sleepily in the sun, and occasionally coming to enough to hook a fish. They never seemed to catch much, but when they did, here's how we broiled them.

Allow about ½ pound of fish per person. Serve with cornbread or spoonbread, broiled tomatoes, some fresh corn on the cob and/or some broccoli.

> *fish up to 3 pounds*
> *salt*
> *lemon juice*
> *pepper*
> *butter*
> *lemon wedges*

Preheat broiler to 450°.

Clean, split and bone fish. Rub very lightly with salt inside and out. Pour lemon juice over it. Sprinkle a bit of pepper on it.

Grease broiler rack, lay fish on it, skin side up, dot with butter. Broil 7 to 10 minutes until fish is flaky. Serve at once with lemon wedges.

POACHED FISH

This is a particularly good way to cook fish fillets that have been frozen.

For 4 people.

> *1½ pounds fish fillets*
> *2 tablespoons butter*
> *1 tablespoon finely chopped onion*
> *1 tablespoon lemon juice*
> *1 cup dry white wine*
> *salt and pepper to taste*

If fillets are frozen, partially defrost and separate. Pat fresh ones dry. Melt the butter in a heavy skillet and sauté the onions until just transparent. Add the fish, pour the lemon juice and wine over them to about ¼" depth. Dash some salt and pepper on them. Let poach uncovered for 3 to 4 minutes on each side or until just flaky. Serve at once.

SAILOR'S FISH STEAKS

Years ago, Dave and I sailed into Cuttyhunk late one afternoon with a lean larder and a yen for lobster. When we had maneuvered ourselves into the dock, old Cap'n. Tilton sadly shook his head as he informed us that there hadn't been a lobster in the pots for 3 days. Faced with the prospect of some canned corned beef hash after a long, hard day at sea, we were devastated, until suddenly Dave spotted a big sea bass hanging on the dock, so freshly caught it was still dripping.

We had a nice big steak cut off it, shoved off to anchor out, fixed a welcome pitcher of martinis, dipped the bass over the side to rinse it, melted some butter in the skillet, poured a bit of lemon juice into it, then sautéed the fish until it was just flaky, added a dash of salt and pepper . . . and feasted.

Try it. Even with a fish steak a few hours out of water. Just be sure no fresh water touches it.

SHAD ROE

Once a year, welcome as a cold beer on the 10th tee, the shad tree bursts into bloom, prophesying the run of the shad up the Bay to spawn, and the arrival of the shad roe on the table. So delicately flavored they need no sauces to help them.

Allow 1 pair of roe per lucky soul.

> *shad roe*
> *bacon strips, 1 or 2 per pair of roe*
> *1 egg, beaten*
> *1 tablespoon water*
> *seasoned powdered breadcrumbs*
> *sliced lemon*

Pat roe dry. Fry bacon until crisp in a heavy skillet, remove and keep warm. Pour off excess fat, leaving only enough to cover the bottom of the skillet well. Beat egg, add water. Season your breadcrumbs with salt and pepper. Dip the roe carefully in the egg; you must not break it. You may find that it is better to put the egg in a deep plate and slide the roe into it. Just as carefully roll them in the breadcrumbs.

Have the fat in the skillet hot, slip the roe in and sauté over medium heat until brown, then turn and sauté other side until brown. Roe will be fairly firm and mealy when done.

Serve with the bacon over them and sliced lemon on the side.

KEDGEREE

A do-ahead casserole. Served with a tossed salad, dry white wine and followed by a pie or pudding, it gives you a simple and complete dinner.

For 6 to 8 people.

> 1 *cup cooked rice*
> 1 *cup cooked white fish or tuna*
> 2 *hardboiled eggs, sieved whites*
> ½ *cup sliced, sautéed mushrooms*
> 2 *tablespoons each minced green pepper and pimiento*

THE SAUCE
> 2 *tablespoons butter*
> 2 *tablespoons flour*
> 1 *cup milk*
> 1 *teaspoon minced onion*
> 1 *teaspoon curry powder*
> 1 *teaspoon lemon juice*
> *salt and pepper to taste*

THE TOPPING
> 3 *tablespoons melted butter*
> 2 *hardboiled eggs, sieved yolks*
> ¾ *cup split salted almonds*

Preheat oven to 350°.

Boil rice, drain and mix while hot with the fish. Sieve the egg whites of the hardboiled eggs. Add the sautéed mushrooms, minced green pepper and pimiento and egg whites to the rice and fish mixture.

Make the sauce by melting the butter in a heavy skillet and cooking the flour in it for 3 to 4 minutes, stirring constantly. Slowly add the milk, stirring constantly until sauce is smooth and thick. Add the minced onion, curry powder and lemon juice. Cook a few minutes, taste and add salt and pepper as needed.

Fold the sauce into the rice and fish mixture, then pour into a greased casserole 12 x 7 x 2".

Make the topping by melting the butter and dribbling over the top of the casserole. Sprinkle the sieved egg yolks on top. Sprinkle the almonds over all.

Casserole is now ready to bake at your convenience. Bake in the moderate (350°) oven for about 30 minutes or until hot, bubbly and browned on top.

SNOW'S CODFISH CAKES

Let's not belabor the niche the cod has created in Massachusetts legend. It was indeed a staple.

For about 12 cakes.

> ½ *pint salt cod (about 1 cup)*
> 1 *pint whole, peeled potatoes*
> *water to cover*
> 2 *tablespoons butter*
> 1 *well-beaten egg*
> *pepper to taste*
> *bacon fat*

Do not freshen the cod. Pick it fine, combine with the potatoes in a heavy saucepan, add the water to cover. Cook covered at a low simmer until potatoes are done. Drain and mash together.

Mix in the butter, the beaten egg and pepper to taste.

Heat enough bacon fat to cover the bottom of a heavy skillet generously, having it hot but not sizzling. Drop the fish mixture off a spoon into the fat and fry cakes until brown, turning once.

Serve hot.

MEATS AND FOWLS

BAKED HAM WITH RAISIN SAUCE

There was always a ham for eating and one still hanging when I was little. And surely, a country ham must be one of man's oldest friends. It keeps for ages, can be fried, ground, until finally the bone makes soup and then goes to a happy dog.

For some, the true, salty country ham is a bit much, but properly prepared it has no equal. Soak as directed, then boil with a cup of sherry in the water for the last ½ hour. Use bourbon if there's no sherry around.

For the more usual smoked ham, proceed as follows:

Soak overnight in apricot or orange juice with ½ cup sherry or bourbon. Place ham fat side up on a rack in a big roaster. Preheat oven to 325°. As ham cooks, baste with the juice, pouring a bit more sherry or bourbon over it from time to time. It should cook from 18 to 20 minutes per pound.

When the ham begins to shrink from the bone, remove it from the oven and trim off the skin. Score the fat and stick whole cloves in it, if desired.

TO GLAZE
½ *cup brown sugar*
1 *teaspoon flour*
½ *teaspoon dry mustard*
dash cloves
dash red pepper
brandy or port

Mix the dry ingredients together and dampen with just enough liquor to make a paste. It should be thick, not runny. Spread the paste over the fat of the ham.

Return to the oven for approximately 20 minutes. Ham will have a beautiful browny gold look.

Allow ham to cool before slicing. It should still be warm, but not fresh from the oven. A country ham should be sliced paper thin. A regular ham should be sliced about as thick as a quarter.

RAISIN SAUCE

Ham's best friend. Try it also on sweet potatoes, omitting the raisins.

Makes about 1½ cups of sauce—for 6 people.

> *ham essence—the drippings in the pan*
> *½ cup brown sugar or ¼ cup brown and ¼ cup white*
> *¼ teaspoon cornstarch*
> *1 cup water*
> *½ cup puffed raisins*

Degrease the ham essence by chilling and removing fat. Dissolve the sugar and cornstarch in a little of the water, then add to the essence with the remainder of the water. Boil down until you have a syrup.

Puff raisins by letting sit in boiling water for about 5 minutes. When sauce is ready, add raisins.

Serve hot.

MOTHER'S HAM ROLLS

An extra-specially good way to serve leftover ham. They go well with sweet potatoes, baked stuffed tomatoes, string beans and slaw.

For 4 to 6 people.

1 *cup ground ham*
2 *tablespoons finely chopped green pepper*
3 *teaspoons prepared mustard*
yeast dough (see Our White Bread, p. 119)
butter

Preheat oven to 375°.

Combine ham, green pepper and mustard into a dryish paste. Roll dough out ¼" thick into a rectangle about 9 x 15". Butter it generously all over. Spread with the ham mixture, then roll it up like a jelly roll, pinching the ends together to seal them.

Slice into 1" pieces and place in a greased flat baking pan. The cut sides of the ends should be face down. Allow to rise until light.

Put into the moderate (375°) oven, then bake the rolls as you would regular ones on the middle rack for about 15 minutes or until done.

HAM CAKES

Another great solution to the leftover ham. (Try stuffed green peppers, too.) Serve these with okra and tomatoes and baked eggplant or corn pudding.

For 4 people.

1½ *cups mashed potatoes*
2½ *tablespoons butter*
1 *beaten egg*
1 *teaspoon chopped parsley*
1 *cup ground ham*
1 *teaspoon finely chopped onion*
2 *tablespoons finely chopped green pepper*
¼ *teaspoon Worcestershire sauce (optional)*
salt and pepper to taste
flour

Boil and mash potatoes, add 1 tablespoon of the butter to them. Beat egg until light, add chopped parsley, potatoes and ham. Mix in onion, green pepper and Worcestershire sauce, if using. Taste for seasoning and add salt and pepper. Since hams vary so in saltiness, you must be quite careful to taste well before adding the salt.

Shape into oval, flat cakes about 3″ long and 1½″ thick. Lightly coat them with flour. Melt the remaining butter in a heavy skillet, using only enough to cover the bottom well and being careful not to burn it; then, over medium heat, sauté the cakes until brown, turning once.

They may be held in a warm oven for a bit.

DAVE'S BEEF STEW

Silas Snow may have been the master of corning beef, but it was not until my husband, Dave, took over the stew pot that this was perfected. It defies description.

For 8 people.

> 2½ *pounds beef (chuck or stew)*
> 2 *tablespoons vegetable or olive oil*
> *garlic salt*
> *salt*
> *pepper*
> 2 *bouillon cubes*
> 6 *cups water*
> 4 *tablespoons flour*
> 3 *tablespoons tomato paste*
> ½ *teaspoon basil*
> ½ *teaspoon thyme*
> ¾ *teaspoon rosemary*
> ½ *cup burgundy*

Cut meat across the grain into bite-size pieces. Sauté in oil, sprinkling lightly with garlic salt, salt and pepper. Dissolve bouillon cubes in 6 cups water. After beef is browned, remove it with a slotted spoon (so that it is drained) to a casserole. Add the flour to the braising juices and brown over high heat, stirring constantly. Add a little of the bouillon water, scraping sides of skillet until all meat bits are in the sauce. Continue to add the bouillon water until used up, then add tomato paste, basil, thyme and rosemary as the sauce boils. When smooth, pour over the meat. Add wine. Cover and cook at a low simmer for 2½ hours or until fork tender.

VEGETABLES

Add the vegetables for the last ½ to ¾ hour, correcting the seasoning. Since this is a great dish for "futures," plan for the exact number of people you expect to feed at one meal. If possible, make the stew the day before, then cook with the vegetables for the last ¾ hour before you plan to serve it. I often make this, freeze half of it for another week, and use half of it.

Allow 1 potato, 2 carrots, 1 medium onion per person. Peel potatoes and quarter. Wire brush carrots clean, trim ends. Peel onions. Drop into the stew.

You may omit the potatoes and serve with rice.

OUR BRAISED BEEF

A very subtle beef stew; try it as an alternate to Dave's Beef Stew. It reheats beautifully—just add a bit more wine if necessary. Serve with rice, a salad, dark bread and burgundy for a feast.

Serves 4 people.

> 1½ *pounds stew beef*
> *lardons of bacon (4–5 slices)*
> *gratings of nutmeg*
> 1 *clove garlic*
> ½ *teaspoon thyme*

½ *teaspoon marjoram*
salt and pepper
peel of 1 lemon
1 *small onion*
¼ *cup olive oil*
4 *tablespoons butter*
flour
herb bouquet: 2 stalks celery, bayleaf, several sprigs
    parsley, pinch of marjoram
1 *cup beef stock*
1–2 *cups boiling water*
1 *cup red wine*

Lard beef with bacon, then cut into bite-size pieces. If using beef that has been already cut up, cut up the bacon and lard the beef. Grate nutmeg, crush garlic, add with the thyme, marjoram, salt and pepper. Chop lemon peel and onion, add. Pour oil in, stir well, let marinate for 2 or more hours, turning meat frequently.

Preheat oven to 325°.

Drain meat. Melt butter in heavy, deep skillet or casserole. Dredge meat in flour and brown in the butter. Add the herb bouquet, stock and enough water to come up about an inch below the top. Cover, cook briskly for 10 minutes.

Add wine. Cook still covered in the moderate (325°) oven for 2–3 hours. After 1½ hours, check for tenderness and to be sure enough liquid remains. Add more water if necessary. Correct seasonings. Meat should be fork tender, so continue to check occasionally, as it may be done sooner than time anticipated.

CAPE COD MACARONI BEEF STEW

Although the last four generations of our Snows have been Berkshire-born, the Snows settled on the Cape in the 17th century, insuring their immortality by ingeniously rigging a ship henceforth called a Snow. This stew harks back to the old seafaring days on the Cape. It is best made a day ahead and reheated.

Serves 8 people.

> 3 *pounds lean shank beef*
> 1 *tablespoon bacon fat*
> 4 *cups tomatoes*
> 1 *medium onion, chopped*
> 1 *tablespoon cider vinegar*
> 6 *whole cloves*
> *salt and pepper to taste*
> 2 *cups cubed potatoes*
> 16-*ounce package macaroni shells*

Cut meat across the grain into bite-size pieces. Heat fat until sizzling in a heavy skillet, then quickly brown the meat. Add tomatoes, chopped onion, vinegar, cloves and several pinches of salt with several dashes of pepper. Cover and simmer slowly for about 2 hours.

When the meat seems to be getting tender, add the cubed potatoes and cook 1 more hour.

Remove both meat and potatoes from the sauce and set aside. Cook macaroni in salted water until half-done. Drain and rinse. Put into sauce and boil for about 4 minutes or until done. Return the meat and potatoes to the sauce, mix well. Correct seasoning.

SNOW FARM SPICED BEEF

At the Farm, even the apple culls were welcome. In the fall they were pressed into sweet cider which was stowed in huge barrels in the root cellar. Much was drunk, but much was left to harden and finally become vinegar for spicing and pickling.

Grandmother Clary could never understand why they seemed so low on vinegar, little dreaming the boys had been tapping the barrels during the hard cider stage.

But she always had enough to spice a bit of beef, an excellent way to help less choice cuts along. This spiced beef makes an unusual buffet supper dish, good with hot rolls and salad.

6 *pounds inexpensive beef*
2 *cups cider vinegar*
water
1 *cup chopped onions*
1 *cup chopped carrots* ·
3 *teaspoons salt*
12 *peppercorns*
1 *stick cinnamon*
12 *whole cloves*
1 *teaspoon allspice (optional)*

Simmer beef in vinegar with enough additional water to cover in a covered pot until almost tender, about 1½ hours. Add all other ingredients, cover and simmer another hour. Remove meat, reserve the liquor. Chop the meat fine. Cook the liquor until it has reduced to about a cup and a half. Correct seasonings. Mix with the meat, pack firmly into greased bread pans. Refrigerate.

Slice thin when cold.

SNOW'S NEW ENGLAND BOILED DINNER

The boiled dinner emerged as naturally from New England cellars as the cranberry from its bogs. Each summer and fall were concentrated, feverish periods of preparation for the long, hard winter ahead. Meat was corned, smoked or hung to freeze. Fruits and vegetables were preserved in as many different ways as possible. Tomatoes, corn, beans, beets were canned, pickled, made into relishes and stored in the pantry.

The root vegetables such as turnips, potatoes, onions, parsnips and carrots along with the pumpkins, apples, cauliflower and even cabbages were stored in the root cellar, a deep dirt room dug into the embrace of the earth. Cool and dark, it stayed at just the right temperature and humidity to keep everything perfectly until the next harvest.

The boiled dinner was the cellar "stew"—turnips, onions,

carrots, potatoes, cabbages—a bit of most everything that had been laid down. Properly done, it is a meal to savor.

For 6 people.

>*5-pound corned brisket of beef*
>*6 peppercorns*
>*1 bayleaf*
>*1 medium-size yellow turnip*
>*6 medium onions*
>*6 carrots*
>*6 medium potatoes*
>*¼ teaspoon allspice*
>*1 head of cabbage*
>*salt and pepper*
>*butter*

Put corned beef, peppercorns and bayleaf in 1½ quarts of water, bring to a boil and simmer covered over low heat for 3 hours.

Pare and cut vegetables into about 12 pieces each. Add turnip and cook 15 minutes. Add all remaining vegetables except the cabbage. Add allspice. Cook 45 more minutes. Add cabbage wedges and boil slowly for 15 minutes. Keep covered always.

Remove beef to a platter and slice against the grain. Surround with the vegetables, pour some of the essence over the whole and serve. Allow each individual to add salt and pepper and butter to taste.

GRANDFATHER CLARY'S CORNED BEEF

Just in case you decide to do your own, here's Grandfather Dwight Elijah Clary's recipe which was written down in 1876, so goodness knows how old it is. My husband's father, Silas, used it at Snow Farm right up until the Second World War. The British Navy used to corn its beef in gunpowder. By Grandfather Clary's time, he'd figured out that it was the saltpeter in the powder that did the trick.

4 gallons of water
7 pounds of salt
3 pounds of brown sugar
3 ounces of saltpeter
1 ounce of soda
100 pounds of beef

Put beef in a large barrel. Heat together all other ingredients and pour over meat. Cover with a wooden lid. Let corn at least six weeks, turning the meat every few days.

OXTAIL RAGOUT

The old farm saying about the hogs, "we use everything but the squeal," applies to the cows also. Our connoisseur friends love this, but you may well hesitate to serve it to new acquaintances unless you've checked first. It's simply the idea, not the taste.

Serve with a hearty bread, a salad and a good burgundy.

For 6 people.

THE STEW
walnut of shortening
5 pounds of oxtails
salt and pepper
4 tablespoons flour
1 quart beef stock or bouillon
2 tablespoons tomato paste
1 teaspoon crumbled basil
½ teaspoon thyme
several sprigs chopped parsley

Use a deep, heavy skillet. Melt shortening and add oxtails. Sprinkle with salt and pepper. Sauté over high heat for 4 to 5 minutes. Remove oxtails with a slotted spoon to a heavy casserole. Stir the flour into the fat in the skillet and brown. Add the beef stock and tomato paste, stirring until smooth and boiling. Add the herbs and chopped parsley. Stir and cook 5 more minutes.

Pour the stock mixture over the oxtails and cook at a low simmer for 2 hours. If you wish, you may cook in a moderate (325–350°) oven for the 2 hours. Place casserole in refrigerator and cool. Degrease.

THE VEGETABLES
6 *whole onions*
1 *dozen whole carrots*

Peel onions, wash and trim carrots. Add to the degreased oxtails and return to stove, cover and simmer for 1 hour or until vegetables are done.

Correct seasoning and serve hot.

STUFFED BEEF HEART

This is a delicious old recipe which came to me from my most gentle cousin Margie Revell Moss, who feeds the birds each morning before she even has her coffee. At Snow Farm, it was also a favorite, cooked much the same.

Serve with rice or boiled, parslied potatoes, green vegetable, and salad, and follow with a pudding.

The amount of stuffing and number of people a heart will serve depends on the size. A calf heart will serve 4, as a rule.

beef, calf or veal heart
fresh breadcrumbs—about ¾ cup
chopped onion—about 3 tablespoons
salt and pepper
about 6 tablespoons butter
¼ cup burgundy wine (optional)

Preheat oven to 325°.

Ask your butcher to clean the heart and remove membranal

tissue. Rinse and dry. Crumble bread, it need not be too fine, add chopped onion and salt and pepper to taste. Melt 2 tablespoons of the butter and mix into the breadcrumbs. Melt another 2–3 tablespoons butter and sauté the heart in it until it turns a bit greyish, turning it on all sides.

Remove heart and stuff it through the opening with the breadcrumb mixture. Skewer it closed. Or slit it, stuff and sew up. Put into a casserole, add a bit of water, a tablespoon of butter, the wine if used, cover and bake in a moderate (325–350°) oven for about 1½ hours or until done.

Slice across as for a jellyroll and serve with essence.

BEEF TONGUE

Hot tongue with horseradish, served on a bed of spinach with some boiled potatoes and a hearty burgundy followed by a good steamed pudding will satisfy the most particular. Plan for 4 to 6 people, and hope for some left over to make a chef's salad or sandwiches the next day.

> 3 *to* 4 *pounds fresh tongue*
> 1 *quart water*
> 1 *bayleaf*
> 8 *peppercorns*
> 3 *whole cloves*
> ⅛ *teaspoon allspice*
> ¾ *teaspoon salt*

Combine all ingredients in a big pot and bring to a boil. Cover, reduce the heat to a simmer and cook for 4 hours.

Remove tongue from the water, skin it, slice and serve nice and hot.

POT HELLION

An unruffled-hostess recipe from my Aunt Mosie's repertoire, this is also economical. Serve with a salad or green vegetable, a hearty wine and follow with baked apples.

Serves 4 to 6

> 4 *tablespoons butter*
> 1½ *pounds ground chuck or round*
> 4 *cups chopped onions*
> 8-*ounce package thin spaghetti* (3¼ *cups*)
> 1 *large clove garlic, crushed*
> ½ *teaspoon Tabasco*
> *several dashes red pepper*
> 3 *cans tomato soup*
> 1 *cup breadcrumbs, rather fine*

Preheat oven to 350°.

Melt 1 tablespoon of the butter in a heavy skillet and brown meat. Reserve. Sauté chopped onions in same skillet, adding more butter if necessary.

Cook spaghetti in well-salted water 8–9 minutes, drain.

Add crushed garlic, Tabasco and red pepper to tomato soup.

Using a buttered casserole, layer the meat first, then the onions, then the spaghetti, making 3 layers of each. Pour the soup mixture over it, spread with breadcrumbs, dot with butter. Bake in the moderate (350°) oven for 45 minutes until browned and buttered.

LAMB SHANKS

Allow one shank per person, unless they are very small. Shanks tend to have a great deal of fat on them, but generally there is enough good, tender meat to satisfy the hungriest man on one shank. And to think people often threw these away!

For 4 people.

TO COOK SHANKS
2 tablespoons vegetable oil
4 lamb shanks
½ teaspoon garlic salt
½ teaspoon salt
¼ teaspoon pepper
1 finely chopped onion
4 tablespoons flour
4 cups lamb, beef or bouillon stock
2 tablespoons tomato paste
½ teaspoon basil
¼ teaspoon thyme
¼ teaspoon marjoram
⅛ teaspoon rosemary
¼ cup burgundy wine

Heat oil in a heavy, deep skillet and have it sizzling. Put shanks in, sprinkle with the garlic salt, salt and pepper. Sauté until nicely browned, remove to a deep casserole. Add finely chopped onion to the shanks.

Brown the flour in the braising oil, add the stock and tomato paste, stirring constantly and cooking until smooth and boiling. Add all the herbs and cook 5 minutes at a low boil. Pour over the shanks and add wine. Cover and cook at a low simmer for 1 hour.

Meanwhile, prepare the vegetables.

TO COOK VEGETABLES
8 to 10 carrots
4 to 6 onions

Clean carrots and leave whole unless very large. Peel onions and leave whole. When casserole has cooked for the 1st hour, add the vegetables and cook another 45 minutes or until tender.

Serve over steamed rice.

BAKED PORK CHOPS

Here's how we get around the usual dry, tasteless pork chop. Stick some potatoes in to bake at the same time, then serve them along with some turnips or greens and applesauce. Allow 1 chop per person as a rule.

> *1½ tablespoons vegetable oil*
> *1″ or more thick pork chops*
> *salt and pepper*
> *tart apples, ½ for each chop*
> *brown sugar*
> *milk*

Preheat oven to 350°.

Heat oil in a heavy skillet until hot almost to the sizzle. Brown the chops quickly in the oil. Remove and place them in a baking dish. Sprinkle with salt and pepper.

Leaving the skins on, slice the apples in half, core and lay skin side down on each chop. Sprinkle with about 1 teaspoon of brown sugar each. Fill the dish with milk almost to the top of the chops. Cover and bake 1 hour or until done.

Check as they bake to be sure milk does not cook away, as it will form a good sauce to pour over them. If sauce seems to be cooking away, reduce the heat and allow a little more baking time, adding more milk if necessary.

SALT PORK AND CREAM GRAVY

Most people seem to think nobody north of the Mason-Dixon line ever ate salt pork. Nothing could be further from the truth. At Snow Farm they not only salted their own pork, but loved it cooked like this for eating with boiled potatoes and a green vegetable. You may wish to try it for breakfast.

After the hogs were killed and hung, the skin had to be debristled. Despite all the special equipment they tried, they found the best debristler was the base of a brass candlestick! It just plain rubbed the bristles off more smoothly, curving into the crannies better. We still have one pair of the candlesticks they used.

After the skin was clean, slabs were cut off the hog down to the real meat. This was the fat with streaks of lean. These slabs were then laid down in plenty of salt—"can't have too much"—and covered with water where it kept indefinitely.

salt pork for 2
2 tablespoons flour
1 cup milk

Trim rind off the salt pork and slice thin, less than ¼″. Fry in a heavy skillet until browned and crisp. Remove and keep warm. Pour off excess fat, leaving about 2 tablespoons. Add flour, cooking until brown. Add warm milk, stirring constantly until smooth and boiling. Serve over the pork.

In Maryland, we just ate it like bacon.

VEAL KIDNEY CHOPS

When mother was a girl, these were a Sunday breakfast dish served with hot rolls and hominy. Staggeringly expensive today, you'll probably want to have them for dinner. Hominy and hot rolls still go well, with baked tomatoes and a green vegetable. You'll want a red wine.

These have to be specially cut, as chops and kidneys are sold separately today. Ask your butcher to cut them about ¾ to an inch thick with the kidney attached. He will want to remove the fat and roll the chop around the kidney, but don't let him. You need the fat to keep the chop from being dry and to give it more flavor.

The veal sold today is often a pinky red instead of whitish. If yours is, then soak it in milk or lemon juice for an hour or so before cooking.

For 2 people.

> 1 *tablespoon butter or bacon fat*
> 2 *veal kidney chops*
> *salt and pepper to taste*
> 2 *tablespoons seasoned flour*
> 1 *cup water or beef stock*

Have a heavy skillet sizzling hot, drop in the butter or bacon fat and let it just melt. Sear the chops quickly on both sides. Lower heat, sprinkle salt and pepper on the chops, cover and let steam about 20 minutes or until done. The chops should be moist and tender when ready.

Remove chops from skillet and keep warm. Season the flour with salt and pepper, then add to the fat and cook, stirring constantly until golden brown. Add water or stock and, stirring constantly, bring to a boil, making a smooth, rich gravy. Correct seasonings.

Return chops to the gravy and let heat well. Serve at once.

You may cook plain veal chops this way also.

KIDNEYS SAUTÉED IN BOURBON

Our pet Sunday brunch dish, this also makes a good and unusual buffet supper offering. For brunch, serve with grits or over toast points, scrambled eggs with fresh chives and hot biscuits. These will keep in a chafing dish. They also may be made ahead and reheated. Allow 1 veal kidney or 3 lamb kidneys per person.

For 2 people.

> 2 *veal kidneys or 6 lamb kidneys*
> 1½ *tablespoons butter*
> 2 *tablespoons chopped onion*
> 2 *tablespoons flour*
> ½ *to ¾ cup bouillon*
> 1 *teaspoon bourbon or to taste*
> *chopped parsley*

Clean and slice kidneys. Drop into cold, salted water for 15 minutes to draw blood if desired. Melt butter in a heavy skillet. Chop onions and sauté.

Add kidneys, cook 5–7 minutes until they have turned brownish. Push aside, add flour, stirring in juice constantly and cooking rapidly for several minutes. Have bouillon warm and add gradually, continuing to stir until you have a smooth, thickened sauce. Add bourbon and boil for about 2 minutes, stirring kidneys into sauce as you do.

Add finely chopped parsley when ready to serve.

MADRAS LAMB OR CHICKEN CURRY

Everyone in the family has decided opinions on curry. This is my favorite. It does take a bit more time, but is worth it. The condiments (boys) are optional in number, but I always serve the fried bananas, chopped egg, coconut and chutney.

For 6 people.

> *6 tablespoons butter*
> *1 crushed clove garlic*
> *1 cup chopped onions*
> *2 tablespoons curry powder, more or less*
> *2 cups chicken stock*
> *½–¾ cups raisins*
> *½ teaspoon ginger*
> *3 tablespoons chopped chutney*
> *8 peppercorns*
> *salt to taste*
> *1 cup coconut milk*
> *2 teaspoons sugar (optional)*
> *1 tablespoon lemon juice*
> *2–2½ cups cooked lamb or chicken*

Use only a wooden spoon with curry preparation, as metal will alter the flavor of the curry.

Melt 4 tablespoons butter in a heavy, deep skillet, add

crushed garlic and sauté. Add chopped onions, cooking until transparent. Soften remaining 2 tablespoons of butter and mix with the curry powder until you have a paste. Add to the onions and swirl in. Pour in chicken stock, add raisins, ginger, chopped chutney, peppercorns and salt. Simmer ½ hour covered.

Taste for the curry and add more if necessary; curry powders vary with type and age. Add coconut milk and mix. Taste for sweetness and add sugar if needed. With canned coconut milk, the sugar will probably be unnecessary. Add lemon juice. Simmer over low heat uncovered until sauce thickens, about 30 minutes. Check for salt and correct if necessary.

Add the cooked meat and simmer slowly until the flavors permeate, about 15 minutes.

Serve over hot rice. If you like, add garlic to the rice water for a heightened flavor.

SUGGESTED BOYS
shredded coconut
chopped hard-boiled egg
chutney
fried bananas (slice, dip in sugar and cinnamon, fry in butter)
diced, fried eggplant (salt slightly, fry in butter)
chopped onion and green pepper
blanched, chopped peanuts or almonds
shredded, toasted codfish
chopped cucumber

MOM BRADLEY'S SCRAPPLE

A favorite of Pennsylvanians and Marylanders, especially Southern and Eastern Shore Marylanders. Originally, scrapple was made from the pork liver and fresh pig's head, but pork shoulder is the "modern" substitute for the head. At least, that's how my great-grandmother made it and how we do it today.

Serve it for breakfast with hominy or grits. I love scrapple sandwiches for lunch or a late snack. To cook, slice ½″ thick, heat in a heavy, ungreased skillet until quite hot, add scrapple and sauté until brown and crisp on both sides.

2 cups waterground cornmeal
2 cups water
2 pounds fresh pork shoulder
4 cups water
salt and pepper to taste
1 pound pork liver
2 teaspoons poultry seasoning
1 teaspoon sage
dash red pepper
¼ teaspoon dried parsley
⅛ teaspoon thyme
pinch marjoram

Mix cornmeal with water, stirring until smooth and free of lumps. Simmer pork shoulder covered in 4 cups of water until tender enough to leave the bone. Salt and pepper to taste. Meanwhile, soak liver in cold salt water to remove the blood. Add to simmering meat and cook until tender, about 30–40 minutes. Do not overcook as liver will become tough.

Remove meat and strain the liquor, skimming off excess fat. Add the soaked cornmeal to the liquor and cook in a double boiler about 1 hour until thick and smooth, stirring from the bottom frequently. Add salt and pepper to taste.

Grind meat and liver with a coarse blade. Add to the cooked hot cornmeal mush, mixing well. Add seasonings. Mixture will be stiff. It is really a highly seasoned cornmeal mush with pork.

Press mixture into loaf pans, and refrigerate until cold. Remove from pans and wrap well. It may be frozen, but tends to get a bit watery. However, it will keep refrigerated for about a week.

FRIED CHICKEN

When we were first married, my New England husband announced that he couldn't stand that awful Southern fried chicken.

And neither can I bear what is palmed off throughout the nation as "Southern" fried. Our way, in use for generations, gives you a tender, moist chicken with the flavor all through it.

For 4 to 6 people.

> 2½- to 3-*pound fryer, cut up*
> ½ *cup flour*
> 1 *teaspoon salt*
> ¼ *teaspoon pepper*
> ½ *teaspoon curry (optional)*
> ½ *cup milk or as needed*
> *butter*

Preheat oven to 350°.

Cut up chicken and pat dry. Mix flour, salt, pepper and curry in a bag. Dip the chicken in the milk, then shake it in the bag, a few pieces at a time, until coated.

Melt enough butter to lightly coat the bottom of a heavy skillet and quickly brown the chicken in it. Melt additional butter in a small pan, about 4 tablespoons.

Use a flat baking pan large enough to hold all the chicken without piling it up. Place chicken skin side down in the pan, pour the melted butter over it and bake on the lower rack of the oven for about 25 minutes. Baste and turn it. Bake another 35 minutes, or until browned and done.

TO COOK ON TOP OF STOVE

Follow the same preparations. Place the chicken in the heavy, greased skillet and brown it over low heat. Cover and steam until almost done, about 1 hour and 10 minutes. Remove cover, raise heat and let crisp for 10 minutes.

STEAMED CHICKEN

Here's how we prepare chicken to use in chicken almond, salads, creamed chicken, etc. The stock is reserved for use in other dishes or added to the bits and bones for soup or more stock.

2½ - *to 3-pound fryer*
2–3 *stalks of celery with tops, chopped*
1 *large onion, chopped*
salt and pepper or poultry seasoning
1 *cup water*
1 *chicken bouillon cube*

Stuff the chicken with the chopped celery and onion. Sprinkle with salt and pepper or poultry seasoning. Wrap it in foil, carefully but not worrying about minor leakage. Bring water to a boil in a heavy pot, dissolve bouillon cube in it, reduce heat and lay chicken in it. Steam slowly over very low heat until done, about 50 minutes.

CHICKEN ALMOND

An old favorite, this has been brought to contemporary perfection by my mother. It makes an excellent entree for 4, can be made ahead if you like, then heated over a double boiler. And it freezes well. Chicken almond begs for a crisp salad and a green vegetable such as string beans and okra.

You may also substitute shrimp for chicken.

2 *cups steamed, cut up chicken (p. 76)*

THE SAUCE
2½ *tablespoons vegetable oil*
¾ *cup each chopped green onions, green pepper, celery*
¼ *cup chopped mushrooms, fresh or canned (optional)*
1 *cup chicken broth*
4 *teaspoons cornstarch*
½ *teaspoon salt*
4 *tablespoons water*
1 *tablespoon soy sauce*

Heat the oil in a large, heavy skillet, adding onions, green pepper and celery, with mushrooms if used, and sautéing until the onions are tender.

Blend the chicken broth with the cornstarch, salt, water and soy sauce until smooth, then stir into the vegetables. (If you have used canned mushrooms, use ¼ cup of their juice with ¾ cup of the chicken broth.) Heat to the boiling point and allow to thicken slightly, continuing to stir.

Add the cut up chicken. Allow to heat through.

THE TOPPING AND ACCOMPANIMENT
½ *tablespoon vegetable oil*
½ *cup roasted almonds*
¼ *cup sliced water chestnuts (optional)*
heated chow mein noodles

Preheat oven to 275°.

Ten to 15 minutes before serving time, put oil in a flat pan and add almonds, roasting until lightly browned. Slice water chestnuts if planning to use. Heat noodles.

TO SERVE

When chicken is hot and topping and noodles are ready, put noodles on plate or platter, top with chicken, spread almonds and water chestnuts over it and serve at once.

SINGAPORE CHICKEN

Mosie is my trunk-aunt. Married to a naval officer, she settled down for two years here and two years there everywhere from Panama to the Philippines, carrying with her little more than a trunk, it always seemed to me. That trunk was stuffed with "Mosie" things, such as Chinese silk paintings, Moroccan hassocks, enormous Indian brasses, all of which transformed mundane furnished apartments into chic, personal homes in two days.

Her efficiency extended to the kitchen where she seemed to spend five minutes muttering incantations in the morning that became superb meals appearing suddenly at dinner.

This is one of her sleight-of-hands. Serve it with baked tomatoes, a tossed salad and hot bread. You may do it all ahead, just placing the casserole in the oven when you wish.

For 4 to 6 people.

½ *cup flour*
½ *teaspoon salt*
¼ *teaspoon pepper*
3½ *-pound cut up fryer*
3 *tablespoons butter*
1 *package frozen Italian beans or snow peas, thawed*
⅓ *cup chopped onion*
1 *can cream of chicken soup*
⅓ *cup milk*
2 *tablespoons soy sauce*
2 *tablespoons finely chopped chutney*
½ *teaspoon ground ginger*
3-*ounce can chow mein noodles*

Preheat oven to 350°.

Combine flour, salt and pepper in bag and shake chicken pieces a few at a time until coated. Heat butter in large skillet and brown chicken.

Remove and place in greased 2-quart casserole. Put thawed beans over chicken. Sauté onion in remaining butter for about 3 minutes or until transparent. Add soup, milk, soy sauce, chutney and ginger to the onion. Heat the mixture to the simmer and allow to simmer about 1 minute, being sure to scrape sides of skillet thoroughly to get all the bits of chicken up.

Pour the sauce over the chicken, cover and bake in the moderate oven (350°) for 1 hour. Uncover, sprinkle with noodles, bake 10 more minutes or until lightly brown.

BROILED HERBED CHICKEN

This is my pet quick and easy dinner that will take care of 2 unexpected guests. Serve it with baked sweet potatoes and tomatoes or succotash and a salad. Use a dry white wine. If you have no guests, save the remainder for the next day's lunch.

For 4 people.

> 2- to 2½ -pound fryer, quartered
> ¾ stick butter
> several large sprigs parsley
> 1½ teaspoons thyme
> salt and pepper
> up to 2 tablespoons vegetable oil

Preheat oven to 350°.

Lift the skin of the chicken carefully with your fingers, being careful not to tear it or detach it except from the main part of the flesh. You are forming pockets in it. Soften butter. Chop parsley and blend it in until you have a slightly greenish paste. Add thyme.

Smear the paste all over the flesh of the chicken under the skin until you have a good, thick coating. Fold the skin back into its normal position and press firmly. Sprinkle the chicken with salt and pepper.

Place chicken on rack in broiling pan wrong side up, place on middle rack and cook for 20 minutes basting with oil once. Turn it, baste again and continue to cook for another 20 minutes, basting with juices and additional oil if necessary. It will be crisp and brown when done.

CREAMED CHICKEN

What a shame creamed chicken has fallen into disrepute as a "ladies' luncheon" dish. It's a hearty, good entree for the family or a dinner party. Steam a chicken (p. 76) or use leftover roast chicken. You will need 2 cups of sauce for each 2 cups of chicken. Serve with a salad, hot rolls and rice.

For 4 people.

    2 cups cooked, cut up chicken

THE SAUCE
(makes 2 cups)
    4 tablespoons butter
    4 tablespoons flour
    1 cup milk
    ¾ cup chicken stock
    ¼ cup mushroom juice
    1 tablespoon chopped parsley
    1 tablespoon chopped sweet pickles
    1 tablespoon chopped pimientos
    ½ cup chopped mushrooms
    splash of pickle juice
    dash of celery salt
    dash of paprika
    salt and pepper to taste
    1 tablespoon dry sherry or vermouth
    ¾ cup cooked peas (optional)
    2 hard-boiled eggs (optional)

Melt the butter in a large, heavy skillet over moderate heat, then add flour and cook, stirring constantly, for about 3–4 minutes, being careful not to burn. Slowly add milk, chicken stock and mushroom juice, stirring constantly as you do, until you have a smooth, thick sauce. It will have a richer color than the pasty white one which has helped ruin this dish's good name.

    Add the chopped parsley, sweet pickles, pimientos and mushrooms with the pickle juice and seasonings. Cook only until flavors are blended over low heat or transfer to the top of a double boiler and cook over simmering water. Add the chicken and the sherry or vermouth. Add peas if desired.

At serving time, slice hard-boiled eggs on top if using.

This may be kept in a chafing dish or over warm water. If it is held over warm water too long, it sometimes will get watery.

CHICKEN SALAD

Steam a chicken (p. 76) or use the leftover roast chicken for this cool delight. Fill half an avocado with it, top with a dollop of mayonnaise and a ring of green pepper, place on a bed of lettuce and surround with freshly sliced tomatoes. Add a hearty, toasted bread and a chilled white wine.

For 2 people.

> 1 *cup cold, cut up chicken*
> ⅛ *cup well chopped onion*
> 1 *tablespoon finely minced parsley*
> ¾ *cup mayonnaise or boiled dressing (p. 109)*
> *celery salt to taste*
> *salt to taste*
> *paprika*

Cut chicken in small pieces, using both white and dark meat if you can. Mix in the chopped onion, minced parsley and dressing. Season with the two salts to taste, sprinkle with paprika and let stand for half an hour so flavors permeate.

TURKEY RÉCHAUFFÉ

My great-aunt Lorraine was sleekly elegant with a most nonchalant manner. She always seemed to have just returned from some exotic spot, and I always thought of her spending her life drifting down some tropical river sipping champagne.

It came as a shock to discover that she had conquered the problem of the leftover turkey.

For 8 people.

> 4 tablespoons butter
> 1 cup sliced mushrooms
> 2 tablespoons flour
> 1½ cups beef broth
> ¼ cup sherry
> 1 cup scalded light cream
> 1 teaspoon grated onion
> salt and pepper to taste
> 3 well-beaten egg yolks
> 3 cups cooked, cut up turkey
> toast points

Melt 2 tablespoons of the butter in a small skillet and sauté the mushrooms until lightly brown. Set aside.

Melt the other 2 tablespoons of butter in a large, heavy skillet and add flour, stirring constantly and cooking 3 to 4 minutes. Gradually add the broth and sherry, continuing to stir and cook gently until smooth and thick. Add the scalded cream, grated onion and salt and pepper to taste.

Beat egg yolks until creamy. Blend a little of the hot sauce into the yolks, beating as you pour, then return the blend to the remainder of the sauce, continuing to beat hard.

Add the cut up turkey and the browned mushrooms and allow them to heat through.

Serve bubbling hot over the toast points.

STUFFED GUINEA HEN

Remember, the guinea hen is not a fat bird and needs basting attention or else it will be too dry.

For 4 people.

> 2½ - to 3-pound guinea hen
> bread stuffing (p. 142)
> salt
> 3 tablespoons melted butter
> 2 tablespoons flour
> bacon or lean salt pork
> ¼ cup chicken fat or drippings and water

Preheat oven to 425°.

Rinse and pat bird dry. Stuff lightly and truss. Rub with salt. Melt the butter and mix with the flour until you have a paste. Spread over the bird. Lay strips of bacon or salt pork over the breast. Dredge roaster with flour.

Place breast side up in roaster and put into 425° oven for 15 minutes until browned. Reduce heat to 375° and continue to cook for 45 minutes or until done, basting about every 10 minutes with the fat or drippings mixed with a little water.

DAVE'S ROAST STUFFED DUCK

It's been said by experts that this is the best roast duck ever . . . succulent without being greasy. Serve with rice. Duck can handle the more definitely flavored vegetables such as turnips or broccoli and likes condiments such as spiced pears. It needs a full-bodied red wine.

For 4 people.

> 3- to 4-pound duck
> 1 orange
> 4 cups breadcrumbs
> water
> ½ teaspoon sage
> ¼ teaspoon thyme
> ¼ teaspoon dill

1 *tablespoon finely chopped parsley*
¼ *teaspoon salt*
¼ *teaspoon pepper*

Preheat oven to 350°.

Rinse and pat duck dry. Cut orange in half and dice half of it with the skin on, being careful to save the juice. Mix the orange and juice with the breadcrumbs adding only enough water to create a bind without making the crumbs gluey. Toss the herbs in, mixing very lightly. Stuff the duck, do not pack it. Truss, rub with an additional sprinkle of salt and pepper. Place on a rack in a roasting pan breast side up.

Cover and cook in moderate (350°) oven for 15 minutes. Remove the cover. Slice the remaining half an orange and layer on the breast of the duck. Return to the oven uncovered and cook for 1 hour and 20 minutes or until done. Remove from the roaster, set on a platter and return to the oven set at warm until sauce is made.

THE SAUCE
1½–2 *cups giblet stock*
1 *tablespoon duck fat*
3 *tablespoons flour*
giblets
¼ *teaspoon each salt, rosemary, thyme*
⅛ *teaspoon pepper*
¼ *cup red wine*

To make stock: When duck goes into the oven, put neck, gizzard, heart and liver in 3 cups of water, cooking covered over a low heat for 1 hour. Throw away the neck, chop up the giblets fairly fine and return to the stock. Hold on warm burner until ready to use.

After duck has been cooked and set on its platter, drain the roasting pan of all but 1 tablespoon of the grease. Quickly brown the flour over high heat in the grease, being careful not to burn, and stirring constantly. Slowly pour in the giblets in the stock, stirring until smooth and at the simmer. Add herbs, salt and pepper and wine. Cover and simmer for 15 minutes. Correct seasoning.

Serve very hot.

FRIED RABBIT

Great-uncle Cliff was quite a hunter, keeping grandfather supplied with rabbit when mother was growing up. It was a much beloved weekly meal. Now, many markets sell dressed rabbit, which does make life easier.

For freshly killed wild rabbit, skin and clean, then wash very thoroughly in water to which vinegar has been added. Put into tepid water and soak for several hours, piercing any blood clots to draw off the blood.

Cut up meat and boil for 10 minutes. Drain. When cool, roll in beaten egg, then in fine, seasoned breadcrumbs.

Melt bacon fat or shortening in a heavy skillet and fry pieces until brown all over. Cover and allow to simmer slowly until tender. Remove from pan and keep warm. Make a gravy by adding flour to the cooking juices in the pan, being sure it cooks several minutes. Add warm milk, salt and pepper to taste, continuing to cook and stir until smooth and rich.

Serve over the rabbit with mashed potatoes.

ROAST VENISON

Venison, like all red meats, must be well-hung to be good. I think many of the failures with game cooking stems not from the method but from the meat. If you're lucky enough to come by a hunk of venison for a roast, soak it in buttermilk and cider vinegar or red wine for 2 days, turning it frequently. This may be done in the refrigerator.

Then lard it with bacon, rub with salt and pepper and roast

as you would beef, basting with a little wine. Start in a hot (400°) oven for about ½ hour, then turn the oven down to 350° for the remainder of the time necessary, depending on the size of the roast.

WILD DUCK

If you're fortunate enough to have some given to you, let's hope they arrive all picked and drawn too. Then just wipe them off with a damp cloth.

Serve duck with wild rice, a good salad and a fresh vegetable. Mix a bit of currant jelly with a bit of port wine to go with it.

Allow 1 duck for each 2 people.

Preheat broiler to 400°. If broiler does not accommodate the size, preheat oven to 500°.

Stuff cavity with a sliced apple and onion. Rub it with a little salt and pepper. Put some butter over it. Layer slices of bacon across the breast.

Place duck breast-side up on a flat broiler pan without a rack. Stick it in the preheated broiler or oven and let it begin to cook, about 10 minutes. Pour about ¼ cup of red wine over it and continue to baste every 5 minutes with the wine and drippings.

Allow to cook about 25 to 30 minutes, watching very closely if using the broiler. It will be brown and tender, and you will be able to wiggle the wings when it is done.

VEGETABLES

FRIED APPLES

You need firm, tart apples, as with all apple recipes. Allow 1 large apple for 2 people. Serve these with pork or for breakfast with sausage and eggs.

> *apples*
> *lemon juice (allow about 1 tablespoon for 2 apples)*
> *bacon fat*
> *sugar*

Stem apples and slice about ¼″ thick. Pour lemon juice over them. Have bacon fat enough to cover bottom of heavy skillet sizzling hot. Place slices in skillet and sprinkle a little sugar on each. Fry 4–5 minutes on each side.

BROCCOLI MARYLAND

Such a poor, mistreated vegetable! Often overcooked, seldom flavored properly, too many times dependent on the Hollandaise to make it palatable. It's so simple.

> *broccoli*
> *1½ cups water*
> *2 teaspoons lemon juice*
> *several chopped celery tops*
> *salt and pepper to taste*
> *butter*

Trim ends off broccoli and set heads down in cold, salted water for 15 minutes. Drain.

Use a heavy saucepan in which the broccoli can stand up. Put in all ingredients except the butter, cover and cook at the simmer for 15 minutes. Drain, correct seasoning, add dabs of butter and serve.

HOLLANDAISE SAUCE
4 tablespoons butter
juice of 1 average lemon
2 beaten egg yolks
¼ cup cream

Melt the butter in the top of a double boiler. Add the lemon juice and well-beaten egg yolks. Stir constantly as the sauce thickens, then gradually add the cream, continuing to stir. The water should be only at a simmer, and a wire whisk is advisable.

CREAMED CELERY

A refreshing change, particularly good with fowl.

4 cups diced celery
salted water
2 tablespoons melted butter
4 tablespoons flour
3 cups warm milk
1 teaspoon salt
pepper to taste

Dice celery, being sure strings are removed. Boil covered in salted water to cover until tender. Drain, save the essence for soup.

Melt the butter and cook the flour in it over medium heat, stirring constantly for about 3 to 4 minutes. Slowly add the warm milk, continuing to stir until you have a smooth, thick sauce. Add the celery and salt. Correct the seasoning to taste, adding the pepper.

CORN ON THE COB

It might seem superfluous to include corn on the cob in a specialty cookbook, but we do cook ours differently, and friends always ask how we do it.

The first rule is: the fresher the better. Pick it yourself, if you can, and race for the kitchen. Put the kettle on with plenty of water—about half full. Then shuck the corn.

Add a tablespoon of salt, a teaspoon of sugar and ½ cup of milk to the water.

When it begins to boil, toss in the corn, cover and let it go about 8 to 10 minutes. Watch it, as the milk may make it boil over and you'll have to set the lid a bit askew.

Serve at once with plenty of butter, salt and pepper.

SOUTHERN FRIED CORN

Allow ½ to 1 ear of corn per person, depending on the size.

fresh corn
chopped green pepper
butter
salt and pepper to taste
several sprigs chopped parsley

Cut kernels off the cob. Depending on the amount of corn you plan to fry, chop enough green pepper to amount to a tablespoon per ear if you're using the pepper.

Melt enough butter to cover the bottom of a heavy skillet, and add a little bit of water, so that the butter and water can simmer. Add the corn, the green pepper if using, salt and pepper to taste, chopped parsley.

Cook until tender, about 5 to 6 minutes, stirring around as it cooks.

CORN PUDDING I

A heavenly dish, much neglected. This is my mother's version, which is rich and a great party dish. It may be made with fresh or canned cream-style corn.

Serves 6 people.

> 2 *tablespoons butter*
> 2 *tablespoons flour*
> 1½ *cups milk*
> 1 *teaspoon salt*
> 1 *beaten egg*
> 2 *cups corn (fresh or canned)*
> 1 *teaspoon Worcestershire sauce*
> ¼ *teaspoon dry mustard*
> *dash of pepper*
> 1 *teaspoon chopped parsley (optional)*
> 1 *tablespoon minced green pepper (optional)*
> *fine breadcrumbs*
> *additional butter*

Preheat oven to 350°.

Melt butter in a heavy skillet and add flour, stirring constantly while you cook it 3 to 4 minutes. Add milk slowly, stirring constantly until you have a smooth, thick sauce. Add salt.

Combine beaten egg with corn, seasonings and optional ingredients, if using. Butter a casserole dish. Blend sauce with the corn mixture and pour in.

Sprinkle breadcrumbs on the top, dot generously with butter. Set in a pan with enough water to cover the bottom. Bake in moderate (350°) oven for 25 to 30 minutes until set. A silver knife inserted in the center should come out clean when it is done.

Serve at once.

CORN PUDDING II

This is a custard-type pudding and is simpler to make.

Serves 6 people.

>   3 *beaten eggs*
>   2 *cups milk*
>   ½ *teaspoon salt*
>   ½ *teaspoon sugar*
>   2 *to* 2½ *cups fresh or canned cream-style corn*

Preheat oven to 350°.

Beat eggs until light. Mix with milk, salt and sugar. Add the corn. Grease a casserole and pour in. Set in a pan of water and bake in moderate (350°) oven for 1 hour. A silver knife inserted in the center should come out clean when it is done.

Serve at once.

SUCCOTASH

Best made with fresh corn, but a good way to use leftover corn or canned, whole-kernel corn. If you're using fresh corn, remember to scrape the cob so you get the milk but not the chaff. Since succotash reheats so well, you may well want to double the quantity and serve again another day.

For 4 people.

>   2″ *piece lean salt pork*
>   2 *cups water*
>   1 *pound lima beans (about 1 cup)*
>   2 *ears corn (about 1 cup)*
>   1 *tablespoon milk*
>   ½ *teaspoon sugar*
>   *salt and pepper to taste*
>   1 *tablespoon butter*

Simmer salt pork in 2 cups of water for about 20 to 30 minutes. Add the beans, cooking until tender, covered.

Cut corn off cob and soak in the milk while the beans are cooking.

When beans are almost tender, add the corn and the seasonings, simmering covered for 10 minutes. Add butter.

CABBAGE AND CORNMEAL DUMPLINGS

When the frost had put summer to sleep, turning the leaves gold and red, it was hog-killing time, time to have cabbage and cornmeal dumplings for dinner on the Eastern Shore. Years after the farm was gone, my great-grandmother continued to serve this for Saturday night dinners, usually followed by an apple pie.

Try cornmeal dumplings in soups, too.

FOR DUMPLINGS
1 *cup cornmeal*
1 *teaspoon salt*
4 *tablespoons shortening*
1¼ *cups boiling water*
10 *tablespoons flour*
2 *teaspoons baking powder*

FOR CABBAGE
3″ *piece lean salt pork*
quart of water
head of cabbage, quartered
salt and pepper to taste

Mix the cornmeal with salt and shortening. Pour the boiling water over the mixture, stirring thoroughly to remove lumps. Let stand until meal swells, about an hour.

Meanwhile, put salt pork into a quart of water and let boil until tender.

Your total cooking time of the cabbage and the dumplings

will be 30 minutes. The cabbage must cook 10 minutes before the dumplings are added, with salt and pepper to your taste added before the dumplings. The dumplings will take 20 minutes to cook and the dish must be served at once, so take heed and plan ahead. When ready, drop cabbage into salt pork water.

Proceed with preparation of dumplings. Sift flour with baking powder, then mix into the cornmeal. Mold into oblong dumplings, using about a heaping tablespoon for each one. (If mixture is too dry, add a bit of milk.) Drop the dumplings as fast as possible into the boiling meat and cabbage, trying to place them on top of the cabbage, not down in the liquor.

Adjust the heat to a slow boil that will not go dry, cover tightly and cook 20 minutes without peeking.

Serve at once.

EGGPLANT—BAKED, FRIED OR BROILED

TO BAKE

Good for a party as well as the family. Serve with fish or fowl or good red meat.

1 *fresh eggplant*
1 *beaten egg*
1 *tablespoon water*
½ *teaspoon salt*
⅛ *teaspoon pepper*
crackermeal or powder breadcrumbs
2 *tablespoons melted butter or vegetable oil*

Preheat oven to 300°.

Wash, peel and stem eggplant. Slice crosswise thin as a dime. Put in a bowl and weight it, leaving for about an hour to remove excess water.

Beat egg, add water, salt and pepper. Dip each slice into the egg, then into the crackermeal. Grease a flat baking dish, layer the slices in it. Pour the melted butter or oil over the top. Bake in the slow oven uncovered until brown, about 30 minutes.

TO FRY

Follow same procedure. Heat butter or margarine in a heavy skillet until quite hot but not sizzling. Fat should not be deep, but a bit more than enough to cover the bottom. Fry slices, turning once. They should be golden brown. Drain them on brown paper in a warmed oven.

TO BROIL

Follow same procedure. Grease broiling pan rack and place on it. Pour a little oil on each slice. Broil at 375° to 400°, watching closely and turning once. The slices will be golden brown and will not need draining.

GREENS—TURNIP, COLLARD AND KALE

These are all old standbys and so good, as they have much more flavor than spinach. They are increasingly difficult to get unless you grow your own. Serve with vinegar or salt and pepper and butter. Keep the liquor for soups, but use sparingly as it is strong. Crumble cold cornbread or spoonbread into it.

Wash and pick over carefully, removing very heavy stems.

Boil a piece of salt pork or hambone in salted water for 15 minutes. Drop greens in and cook until done, about 20 minutes.

BAKED ONIONS

Depending on the size of your onions, allow 1 to 3 per person.

onions
salt
pepper
butter

Preheat oven to 325°.

Boil onions until half done. Place right-side up in a shallow casserole. Sprinkle with salt, a dash of pepper and ½ pat of butter per onion. Add just enough of the essence water onions were cooked in to cover bottom of pan.

Bake in a moderate (325°) oven for approximately 25 minutes. Time will depend on size of onions.

BOILED OKRA

We serve this both as a vegetable and as an hors d'oeuvre. Allow six or seven pods per person either way.

AS A VEGETABLE

Wash whole young tender pods, place in boiling salted water. Cook 10 minutes after water returns to the boil. Remove at once and serve with melted butter, salt and pepper.

AS AN HORS D'OEUVRE

Cook as above, serve with Hollandaise sauce (p. 89). Allow ¼ cup of sauce for each 7 pods. Pods are picked up by the stem.

OKRA AND TOMATOES

I was weaned on this and adore it. Since my husband won't even look at okra, its omission from my menus has been one of the tragedies of my married life. Its colorful red and green adds a fillip to the looks of a dinner.

For 6 people.

2 cups tomatoes, fresh or canned
2 slices crumbled white bread
½ teaspoon salt

    1 *tablespoon sugar*
    dash of pepper
    ½ *stick of butter*
    10–12 *pods okra*
    ear of corn (optional)

Peel tomatoes if fresh. Stew tomatoes in skillet until juice has boiled down somewhat. Crumble bread thoroughly and stir in. Add seasonings and butter, cooking until mixture begins to thicken. Slice okra about 1″ thick and add, continuing to cook until the okra is tender, about 10 minutes. The total cooking time will be about 35 minutes.

    If using corn, add to the pot 5 minutes before adding the okra.

OKRA AND STRING BEANS

The okra gives a different, quite delicious flavor to the string beans, rather like that of haricots verts.

For 4 people.

    2″ *piece lean salt pork*
    4 *cups water*
    1 *pound string beans*
    10 *pods okra*
    pepper to taste
    salt to taste
    butter

Boil lean salt pork in the water, covered, until flavor has been extracted, about 15 to 20 minutes. Trim ends of beans and okra. Add the beans to the water and cook covered for 10 minutes at a low simmer.

    Add the whole okra and cook another 10 minutes, or until both vegetables are tender. You may add some pepper with the okra. Correct the seasoning after cooking.

    Drain and serve with butter.

FRESH PEAS AND DUMPLINGS

I always thought peas 'n' dumplings were one word and am still not sure they shouldn't be. When I used to have the duty of shelling peas, mother always had to admonish me not to eat them all before they're cooked. Just off the vine, peas are so sweet raw, it does seem a shame to cook them!

For 4 people.

> 2″ *piece lean salt pork*
> 2 *cups water*
> 2 *pounds fresh peas*
> ½ *teaspoon salt*
> ½ *teaspoon sugar*
> 2 *tablespoons butter*

Simmer the salt pork in about 2 cups of water for 15 minutes. Add peas, salt and sugar. Simmer 10 minutes and add dumplings. Peas should cook 20 to 25 minutes only, and be nice and firm. Butter is added before serving.

FOR DUMPLINGS
This will make about 12 to 15.

> 1 *cup flour*
> ½ *teaspoon salt*
> 2 *heaping teaspoons baking powder*
> 2 *tablespoons lard*
> *up to* ½ *cup milk*

Sift dry ingredients together. Mix in the lard until you have a stiff dough, add a little milk as you mix. Dough must be stiff enough to drop off the end of a tablespoon.

Uncover peas and drop the dumplings in the boiling essence as fast as you can. Cover tightly and continue to boil for 15 minutes without uncovering.

Do be sure that you have enough liquid to boil for that length of time without going dry, as you do not want to uncover while the dumplings are cooking. If you've a question, add more water before continuing and bring to a boil.

Serve at once. Dumplings do not hold well.

STUFFED PEPPERS

When the peppers began to ripen, they arrived en masse like a school of fish. That meant large consumption, and one marvelous way we loved them then (and still do) was stuffed. Here are two recipes. Serve them as an entree with boiled onions, glazed carrots or any compatible vegetable, then follow with a pie.

For 4 people.

METHOD I
4 medium-large peppers
½ cup diced celery
diced green pepper
4 sprigs chopped parsley
1 tablespoon minced onion
2 cups ground cooked ham
½ cup breadcrumbs (or corn or rice)
¼ teaspoon salt
½ teaspoon thyme
dash pepper
1 small pulped tomato (⅛ cup) (optional)

Preheat oven to 350°.

Top, seed and clean peppers. Parboil for 3 to 5 minutes. Be sure they remain crisp enough to handle.

Dice celery and pepper remaining in the tops, chop parsley, mince onion. Mix with the ground ham and all other ingredients.

Stuff the peppers and place in a pan with enough water to cover the bottom. Bake in the moderate (350°) oven for 20 minutes.

Ground beef, cooked and lightly seasoned, may be substituted for the ham.

METHOD II

4 medium-large peppers
⅔ cup saffron rice
1⅔ cups ground ham
2 tablespoons ground salted peanuts
2 chopped green onions
2 stalks chopped celery
salt and pepper to taste
milk
butter

Preheat oven to 350°.

Prepare peppers as in Method I. Saffron rice is made by adding a thread of saffron to the rice water. Don't use powdered saffron.

Mix the rice with the ham, peanuts, onions and celery. Taste for the amount of salt, as your ham may be salty enough. Add pepper. Moisten the mixture with a little milk, adding only enough to give you a slight bind of the ham mixture. Stuff the peppers, place a generous dab of butter on each.

Place in a pan with enough water to cover the bottom and bake in the moderate (350°) oven for 20 minutes.

SAUTÉED SWEET POTATOES

Bake sweet potatoes or use leftover baked ones. Peel and slice about ¼″ thick. Melt butter in a heavy skillet, lay slices in it, sprinkle with salt and pepper, then sauté until crusty on each side, turning once.

ORANGE SWEET POTATOES

As pretty to look at as they are to eat, this is a nifty old-fashioned way to serve sweet potatoes, especially for a buffet.

For 6 people.

> 3 *large oranges*
> 3 *medium-large boiled sweet potatoes*
> 4 *tablespoons butter*
> ½ *scant teaspoon salt*
> ½ *cup orange juice*

Preheat oven to 350°.

Cut oranges in half and carefully extract juice without damaging the skins. Remove the pulp and membrane, so you have 6 shells.

Boil, peel and mash your potatoes. Add butter, salt and orange juice to them, beating until smooth. Fill the orange shells so they heap a bit in the center, dot with butter. You may set these aside until you are ready, if you like.

Place them in a pan and bake in the moderate (350°) oven until heated through, about 15 to 20 minutes, depending on how long you let them cool before baking.

CANDIED SWEET POTATOES

For 4 happy people.

> 2 *large sweet potatoes*
> ⅔ *cup brown or maple sugar*
> ¼ *cup water*
> *dash of salt*
> *dash of cinnamon*
> *butter*

Preheat oven to 350°.

Boil sweet potatoes in their skins until about half done. Peel, slice lengthwise ½″ thick and place in a shallow baking dish.

Make a syrup by combining the sugar, water, salt and cinnamon and boiling slowly until it begins to thicken. Pour it over the potatoes. Dot them generously with butter.

Bake in the moderate (350°) oven about 30 minutes, basting frequently until they have a glaze and are tender.

ESCALLOPED POTATOES

For 6 people.

> 6 *medium potatoes*
> 1 *large onion*
> *salt and pepper*
> 1 *tablespoon flour*
> 3 *cups milk*
> ½ *stick butter*

Preheat oven to 350°.

Peel and slice potatoes thin as a half-dollar. Layer two of them on the bottom of a greased casserole. Slice onion as thin as possible and layer ⅓ of it over the potatoes. Sprinkle with salt and pepper, about ⅛ teaspoon each. Add another layer of potatoes, another of the onion, salt and pepper and repeat for the third layer. Mix the flour with the milk until smooth and pour over. Slice butter thin and layer on top.

Bake in the moderate (350°) oven for 1 hour or until done.

MOSIE'S BAKED SQUASH

For 4 to 5 people.

> 2 *pounds yellow neck squashes*
> 3 *large onions, chopped*
> ¼ *teaspoon salt*
> *gratings of pepper*

¼ cup water
1 can mushroom soup
2 tablespoons butter
2 rounded tablespoons flour
additional ½ stick butter
crusts from 5 slices of bread

Preheat oven to 350°.

Wash and brush squashes vigorously to clean, peeling only if they're old and tough. Cut them up, chop onions and combine in a heavy saucepan with the salt, pepper and water. Cook covered until tender. Drain.

Combine the soup with the butter. Stir in the flour and mix well until smooth. Pour into the squashes and mix. Pour the mixture into a casserole dish.

Melt the ½ stick of butter, break the breadcrusts into small pieces and toss lightly in the melted butter. Spread over the top of the squashes.

Bake in the moderate, preheated (350°) oven about 20 minutes or until browned.

MOM BRADLEY'S SAUTÉED SQUASH

Southern Maryland, cobwebbed with its rivers, creeks, ponds and swamps along the Bay, steams in the summers with air so heavy it seems to perspire. The heavy wood stoves that warmed the kitchens in winter made them unbearable in summer and gave birth to the Summer Kitchen.

Many were large screened porches (as was Snow Farm's for that matter), but Mother's favorite was her grandmother's on the Eastern Shore. Mom Bradley had a huge, brick-floored room in the cellar, cool and dim refuge from the heat. It was a giant, eat-in kitchen with a kerosene stove and a long table that was always set and laden with pickles, jams and condiments under a netting.

Here is one of the dishes she made down there. Vary the amounts for the number of people.

summer squash
bacon grease
sugar
salt and pepper

Wash and brush squash vigorously. Don't peel unless they are big and tough. Slice them thin. Melt bacon grease to cover the bottom of a heavy skillet. Sauté the squashes, stirring and mashing as they cook, until all the water is out. Add a little sugar, salt and pepper to taste.

THE FRESH TOMATO

Whether you start from seeds or buy baby plants, the tomato vine is a joy all summer long. It seems to preen itself in the sun, saying "Look at me, I'm so beautiful!" as it grows into a rampantly luxurious plant, then waves its tiny yellow blossoms and, finally, bends under a rich crop of beautiful red fruit.

I plant tomatoes among my flowers, with chives and garlic and yellow marigolds nearby to repel or trap the insects.

Since we just won't eat the tasteless store-tomatoes available all winter, we gorge ourselves during the summer, canning or freezing what is finally left and frying those that won't ripen.

To savor them at their best right off the vine, slice and sprinkle with freshly chopped basil, and add a dab of mayonnaise or oil and vinegar. We seldom put them in a tossed salad, as they lose their identity and diminish that of the greens.

STEWED TOMATOES

If you've rather avoided stewed tomatoes because they so often seem gelatinous, then you must try our way.

For 4 people.

> 2 cups tomatoes
> tomato juice
> ⅓ stick butter
> 1 slice crumbled white bread
> 3 to 4 tablespoons sugar
> sprinkle of parsley
> salt and pepper to taste
> 1 teaspoon flour

For canned tomatoes: Drain off most of the juice and reserve.

For fresh tomatoes: skin by dropping into boiling water for a minute, then removing and peeling. Quarter, put into a saucepan with the tiniest bit of water, cover and cook over low heat for 15 minutes. Drain off most of the juice and reserve.

Put the tomatoes in a heavy saucepan with the butter, heating until the butter melts. Add the crumbled bread and cook over low heat covered until the mixture is thick and blended, stirring frequently to prevent sticking. Add sugar, parsley, salt and pepper to taste.

Mix the flour with a little bit of the reserved juice until you have a paste, then add to tomatoes. Bring to a boil for a few minutes until thick and creamy. Correct seasonings.

Save the remainder of the juice for soups or just drinking.

BAKED TOMATOES

A quick, easy dish, this is delicious for a party as well as a family standby. Allow 1 generous sized tomato per person or 2 small ones. Use firm, not overly ripe ones.

Cut out stems, making about an inch-wide, funnel-shaped hole. Press fresh, crumbled basil leaves into hole. Add a dash of salt, pepper and a generous amount of brown or white sugar. Put a dab of butter in, then sprinkle more sugar on top. Breadcrumbs may be added before you put in the butter if desired.

Bake about 30 minutes in a shallow pan with a tiny bit of water in it in a preheated moderate (350°) oven.

TO BROIL

Prepare as above and stick under the broiler at 350° for about 20 minutes. Watch closely and adjust heat to prevent burning.

FRIED TOMATOES

Good anytime for slightly underripe tomatoes, this is a pet dish when the first threat of frost snaps the air. I take all the remaining tomatoes off the vines, wrapping them individually in newspaper to ripen. Those that show a tinge of color will ripen gradually over the weeks, as will most of the very green ones showing some white at the stem end. The others are immediate candidates for frying.

As many tomatoes as you want.

> 1 *beaten egg*
> *water*
> *breadcrumbs or cracker crumbs*
> *salt and pepper*
> *chopped parsley*
> *onion juice or onion salt*
> *butter*

Slice tomatoes about ½″ thick. Some tiny ones will be almost whole. Beat egg well and add about a tablespoon of water. Have breadcrumbs powder fine and season with salt, pepper, chopped parsley and onion juice or salt to taste. Dip tomatoes (they should be dry) in egg, then crumbs, repeating if necessary to coat slices thoroughly. Fry in butter over medium heat until tender.

Riper ones will take about 10 to 15 minutes, while the green ones will need 15 to 20, depending on size. Serve at once.

BAKED STUFFED TOMATOES

See Stuffed Peppers recipe (p. 99) and follow it for tomatoes. Hollow out centers of the tomatoes about 1 to 2 inches wide depending on the size. Do not parboil. Use the tomato pulp in the stuffing. Stuffing for 4 peppers will fill about 8 tomatoes. Since these cook down more than peppers, allow 2 tomatoes apiece.

TOMATO ASPIC

A truly marvelous aspic made with tomatoes, not juice. Serves 6 or 7 to 8 with vegetables added to it.

> 1 *small crushed clove garlic*
> 1 *crumbled bayleaf*
> 2 *cups tomatoes*
> 1 *teaspoon salt*
> 1 *teaspoon sugar*
> *dash Worcestershire sauce*
> *dash celery salt (optional)*
> *pinch oregano (optional)*
> *several celery tops (optional)*
> *several chopped basil leaves*
> 2 *tablespoons cider vinegar*
> 1 *scant teaspoon Sure-gel*
> 1 *package gelatin*
> ⅓ *cup water*
> ½ *to 1 cup chopped vegetables (optional)*

Crush garlic, crumble bayleaf and add to tomatoes with the salt, letting sit for 1 hour.

Add sugar, Worcestershire sauce, any or all of the optional ingredients, and the basil. Cook covered at a low simmer until well blended and ready to sieve, about 30 minutes. Add the vinegar and Sure-gel. Sieve. Soften the gelatin in ⅓ cup water and mix in. Pour into mold and set in refrigerator.

If you wish to use vegetables, allow to set until thickened but not jelled. Then mix in any or all of the following: chopped celery, green pepper, grated carrots, shredded cabbage.

YELLOW TURNIPS (Rutabagas)

It's amazing how many people have stopped me in the market to ask timidly how I planned to cook the turnip in my cart, leading me to believe that this is a much-neglected and unappreciated vegetable. It has a hearty, distinctive flavor which is excellent with roast fowl or red meat. It also goes into stews and soups with discretion.

For 4 people.

> *1½ pounds yellow turnips (to make 2 cups mashed)*
> *2 tablespoons butter*
> *½ teaspoon salt*
> *½ teaspoon sugar*
> *pepper to taste*

Pare and cut up turnips. Boil in water to cover until tender, about 45 minutes. Mash, add butter and seasonings. Serve hot. These reheat perfectly.

SLAW AND DRESSING

SLAW

What is commonly served as slaw is a travesty if you've ever had the real thing. The secret is in the cabbage which must be very fresh and sweet and in the dressing which should be a boiled one.

For 6 people.

4 cups shredded cabbage
½ medium green pepper, chopped very fine
several sprigs parsley, chopped very fine
boiled dressing

Shred cabbage into the finest possible slivers. Be sure pepper is finely chopped and that parsley is also. Mix together, add enough boiled dressing to bind it sufficiently. Let stand for 30 minutes before serving. If the flavor is not quite sweet enough, add a dash more sugar.

Slaw will keep in the refrigerator for a day or so.

BOILED DRESSING

This is the *only* dressing for slaw. It is also delicious with cold or hot vegetables and with other salads. My grandmother never ate mayonnaise and used this in all cases where most people used mayonnaise. It is a different, delightful change.

1 egg
1 cup cold water
2 tablespoons sugar
2 tablespoons flour
1 teaspoon dry mustard
dash red pepper
¼ teaspoon salt
cider vinegar
cream or sour cream (optional)

Beat egg and water together. Mix sugar, flour, mustard, pepper, salt together and add to liquid mixture, stirring until smooth. Cook over low heat, stirring constantly until mixture coats a spoon as a custard would.

Add vinegar until dressing is as tart as you like, starting with 1 tablespoon. This should be tart, and, since vinegars vary so, you must proceed to taste. Refrigerate.

When ready to serve, you may thin with cream if you desire.

HOMINY, GRITS
AND SOUFFLES

HOMINY

When the first Richard Mosse landed in Virginia in 1622, he must
have gazed with wonder on the acres of corn, the mother of life,
"she who sustains us," as the Indians called it. And, indeed, it was
this Indian corn that sustained the colonists from the Massachusetts Bay Colony to Jamestown. They had found not only a boun-
tiful source of food, but a whole new way of planting and
cultivation, for the Indians sowed their corn in hills, 4 kernels
"set not to touch," while the Europeans were still using the
scatter method of sowing.

They also learned to plant in rows, to cultivate the weeds
out and to interplant with squashes, 'pompions' and 'Turkie beans'
which produced succoquatash.

Hominy was called Hommony by the English and some tribes
(probably from O-me-nee), Sapaan by the Swedes and other
tribes (from which we undoubtedly get the Long Island name
"samp"), and Sagamité by the French.

By any name, it is the husked whole kernel of the corn, usually dried in wood ash lye to loosen the husks, and, it was thought,
to add calcium. It was called lye hominy right into this century
by my family.

When it was to be used, it was soaked overnight to remove
the lye, then simmered in a black iron pot on the back of the coal
stove until fully expanded—about triple its original size. It was
then drained and sautéed in an iron skillet with a dollop of bacon
fat, salt and pepper. Great-grandmother and grandmother served
it for breakfast with homemade scrapple. Fabulous.

If you cannot find dried hominy or samp, the canned type still made in Baltimore can sometimes be located. It is not as good, but well worth eating. Sauté as above. You may wish to try it with milk and butter also.

GRITS

Much maligned, grits deserve your loving care and an honored spot on the menu in lieu of potatoes or rice. Another legacy from the Indians, grits became popular only in the south for some strange reason, although an indigenous food with most of the tribes throughout the East.

The dried corn kernels (hominy) were put in a little water and allowed to stand until they'd swelled a bit. They were then put into the hollowed-out heart of a tree stump and slowly pounded until the husks separated and could be washed away. Only the coarse-ground grits remained. The ingenious colonists quickly perfected milling to replace this ancient method, being in much too great a hurry to wait for their grits.

What was also called grits back in 1752 emerges as one of our first concentrated foods. The corn was baked in hot sand, ashes or an oven, then pounded until it was of a coarse grits consistency and the hulls washed away. It was then dried and mixed with maple sugar or some such and stored in a sack. On the trail, it was taken out by the handful, mixed with water and perhaps a little bear or deer grease to be cooked as a mush.

Get coarse ground grits if you can find them—very difficult—and if not, regular grits in preference to the quick-cooking kind. Cook according to the package directions.

Serve with butter, salt and pepper or with gravy. For breakfast, try maple syrup.

FRIED GRITS

Serve for breakfast with eggs and meat or alone.

Pour hot leftover grits into a water glass or glass dish which has just been rinsed with cold water. Chill until stiff, usually overnight. Unmold and slice about ⅓″ thick or cut into cakes. Melt bacon grease or butter in a heavy skillet and sauté the cakes a few minutes on each side. Serve at once, while they are crisp and hot.

Grits may be batter-fried, although I rather deplore this. However, you may like them even better. Beat an egg, adding a bit of milk or water to it. Dip slices in, coat with seasoned flour and fry as above. Slices should be slightly thicker for this.

BAKED GRITS

For breakfast, lunch or dinner, these are heavenly. Try them in place of potatoes or pasta. Good for a fast buffet dish.

For 3 to 4 people.

> 1 *cup cooked grits*
> 2 *to 3 tablespoons butter*
> 1 *beaten egg*
> ⅓ *cup milk*
> *salt and pepper to taste*

Preheat oven to 350°.

If you are using hot grits, just beat in the butter until it has melted. If cold grits, melt the butter first. Beat egg, add the milk and mix with the grits. Correct for salt and pepper. Pour into a casserole dish, place in a pan of water and bake in the moderate (350°) oven for 45 to 60 minutes or until puffy and browned on top.

BAKED CHEESE GRITS

Add ¼ cup grated cheddar cheese with the butter and beat in.

GNOCCHI À LA LORRAINE

One of my mother's pet recipes, this is great for parties and sure to convert all those "I hate grits" types. Use this in place of the usual potato and pasta casseroles.

For 12 people.

> 1 *quart milk*
> ½ *cup butter*
> 1 *cup grits*
> 1 *teaspoon salt*
> ⅛ *teaspoon pepper*
> ⅓ *cup grated Parmesan cheese melted with* ⅓ *cup butter*

Bring milk to a boil in the top of a double boiler. Add ½ cup of butter and let melt. Gradually stir in grits, cooking over boiling water covered until well done, at least an hour. Add salt and pepper. Remove from heat and beat until creamy, about 5 minutes in an electric mixer.

Grease a 13 x 9 x 2″ casserole, pour the grits into it and allow to set until cold and firm. Cut into rectangular pieces about ⅜ x 2 or 3″ wide. Place these pieces in a serving casserole that can go into the oven. You may refrigerate until ready.

Preheat oven to 400°, 375° if using glass pan.

Melt the cheese and butter together and pour over the grits. Bake for 30 to 35 minutes. Run under the broiler for a few minutes to give it a crust. Serve at once.

LAURENA'S CHEESE SOUFFLÉ

Laurena. Shaped like a nice, soft pudding, comforting as warm milk, she has been the bulwark of the Annapolis house for over a quarter of a century. For many years I didn't realize that she couldn't read, so blithely had I wandered through the kitchen.

When asked how to make something, she chuckles out a pinch of this and a bit of that, all by eye and by instinct. Now, carefully measured, we have her version of our cheese soufflé.

For 4 or 5. Do not double recipe.

> *4 separated eggs*
> *⅛ stick melted butter*
> *3 tablespoons flour*
> *1 teaspoon mustard*
> *1 teaspoon Worcestershire sauce*
> *¾ cup warm milk*
> *1 cup grated sharp cheddar cheese*

Preheat oven to 325°.

Grease casserole and prepare a paper collar.

Separate eggs, beating yolks until creamy. Melt butter in a heavy skillet and stir in flour, cooking and stirring for 3 to 4 minutes. Stir in mustard and Worcestershire sauce. Warm milk and add gradually, stirring and cooking until you have a smooth, thickened sauce. Add grated cheese and let it melt.

Remove from heat and pour a little at a time, beating constantly into the beaten egg yolks until well blended. Cook for 1 minute over boiling water. Set aside to cool.

Beat egg whites until stiff but not dry. Fold gently into the cooled sauce. Pour into the greased casserole and cut around the collar.

Place in a pan of warm water and bake in the moderate (325°) oven for 1 hour. Serve immediately.

LOIS' DEPENDABLE CHEESE SOUFFLÉ

As nearly as I can determine, variants of this cheese soufflé were the traditional way it was made in the 19th century. Grandmother Clary's used crackers, while Frances Snow's used stale bread-crumbs. Both called them "Cheese Fondue." Similar approaches called them cheese puddings. We call my sister-in-law's version "Dependable."

Serves 12 people.

> 8 *well-beaten eggs*
> 4 *cups milk*
> 1 *teaspoon dry mustard*
> 1 *teaspoon salt*
> 1½ *pounds grated sharp cheddar cheese*
> 9 *to* 10 *slices slightly stale bread*

Beat eggs well, then add milk, mustard and salt, beating again. Grate cheese. Butter the bread and cube it.

Butter a deep casserole dish and put a layer of bread in it, then a layer of cheese, alternating until it is all used up. Pour the egg mixture over it and let stand several hours or overnight.

Preheat oven to 325°.

Place casserole in a pan with a little water and bake for 1 hour.

Serve at once.

BREADS AND GRIDDLE CAKES

CORNBREAD

This is not the dry, crumbly kind of cornbread usually served, but a much more moist and delicate one because of the hot fat. Serve it hot with butter or crisp bacon and hot bacon fat. Serve it cold. Crumble it up in some buttermilk or pot likker and eat it with a spoon.

For 6 people.

> 1 cup waterground cornmeal
> 1½ cups boiling water
> about 5 to 6 tablespoons bacon fat
> 1 cup milk
> 1 egg
> 2 teaspoons sugar
> ½ cup flour
> 2 teaspoons baking powder
> 1 teaspoon salt

Preheat oven to 400°.

Put cornmeal in a mixing bowl and pour the boiling water over it. Let cool if you have time.

Put the bacon fat in an 8 x 8″ pan and stick it in the oven, letting it get sizzling hot.

Add the milk to the cornmeal and mix in. Beat in the egg and sugar. Sift flour, baking powder and salt together and beat into the batter until smooth. Pour in about 2 to 3 tablespoons of the hot fat and mix. Leave the remaining hot fat in the pan, pour in the batter and bake in the hot (400°) oven for 30 to 40 minutes, until browned and bubbly. Cut into squares and serve.

CORNSTICKS

Crunchy, crunchy good, great with fowl, fish or chowders as well as for breakfast. Makes about a dozen 6 x 1½ " sticks in my old cast-iron pan.

> 4 *tablespoons bacon fat*
> 1 *cup waterground cornmeal*
> ¼ *teaspoon salt*
> ¼ *teaspoon soda*
> 1½ *teaspoons sugar*
> 1 *cup buttermilk*
> 1 *unbeaten egg*

Preheat oven to 400°.

Put bacon fat into each section of your stick pan and heat until sizzling hot. Meanwhile, combine cornmeal, salt, soda and sugar. Pour in the buttermilk, stir in the unbeaten egg and beat until smooth.

Pour about half of the hot bacon fat into the batter, leaving a residue in each section of the pan. Stir thoroughly. Fill the sections of the pan three-quarters' full with batter and bake in the hot (400°) oven about 25 minutes or until brown and crisp. Serve hot with butter.

SPOONBREAD

Absolutely the greatest, this is how we've been indulging ourselves for some 100 years. Serve piping hot with plenty of butter. Spoonbread replaces potatoes and such with dinner. It is perfect with fish and seafood dishes.

This was always my father's favorite midnight snack—cold and crumbled into a glass of buttermilk or turnip green likker.

For 5 or 6 people.

> 1 *cup waterground cornmeal*
> 1 *tablespoon sugar*
> 1 *teaspoon salt*
> 1¼ *cups boiling water*
> 2 *slightly beaten eggs*
> 1 *cup evaporated milk diluted* ½ *and* ½
> 3 *tablespoons bacon fat*

Mix cornmeal, sugar, salt and boiling water in a bowl. Let stand 1 to 2 hours. Get eggs out and let come to room temperature.

Add milk and slightly beaten eggs.

Preheat oven to 375°.

Melt the bacon fat in a 1½-quart round baking dish or casserole and pour 2 tablespoons of the fat into the batter, mixing until quite smooth. Leave the remaining fat in the dish and pour the batter into it.

Bake in the moderate (375°) oven for 45 minutes, until browned. Serve as soon as possible.

JOHNNYCAKE

When the Indians introduced the settlers to corn and the meal made from it, they also taught them to make "journey cake." On the trail, the cornmeal was carried in a little sack, then just mixed with water and cooked over an open fire, really a mush. Hence its name.

As time elapsed, the "journey cake" evolved into the more sophisticated johnnycake. Although it is still made at times as a little griddle cake, the Snows have made it like this for many generations. My husband still prefers it to cornbread.

Serve hot with butter and marmalade or jam. It can be reheated in foil or eaten cold.

For 6 to 8 people.

1 *beaten egg*
2 *tablespoons melted bacon fat or butter*
1 *cup cornmeal*
1 *cup flour*
2 *teaspoons baking powder*
¾ *teaspoon salt*
1 *cup milk*

Preheat oven to 375°.

Beat egg until light and drop melted fat into it, stirring well. Sift all dry ingredients together and mix in. Mix in milk.

Grease a flat 8 x 8″ cake pan and bake in the moderate (375°) oven for ½ hour.

Cut into squares for serving.

ANN SANDS' PONE BREAD—1835

Take as much cornmeal as is wanting for use, sift it through a hair sifter; put it in an ironpot, and pour on it boiling water, stir it with a spatula or ladle until it becomes well mixed and quite thick; this being night, let it remain in the same vessel till morning, and if kept warm it will be well fermented (which is necessary), then put it in what is called a Dutch oven, it being hot before the dough is put in it, apply good lives [sic] on the lid of the oven and under it, being careful not to burn the bread. When thus prepared if done carefully and according to this recipe, more wholesome and better bread cannot be used for breakfast. I think it anti-dyspeptic, as no lard or butter is used in preparing the bread, tho' after it is cooked fresh butter adds to its flavor.

OUR WHITE BREAD

When I was growing up, the old-fashioned rhythms of the household were still flowing along just as inexorably as they had when my mother and her mother were growing up. I could tell what day it was by the very smells. Mondays were the clean warmth of ironing. Fridays were pungent wax and fresh flowers. Saturdays were nose-twitching whiffs of baking breads and cakes.

This is our loaf bread, so good that friends ask for a loaf as a present. Eat the first slices hot if you can. It will make a sandwich a whole new experience. And toasted! Freezes perfectly.

Makes 2 loaves.

> 1¾ *cups lukewarm water*
> 2 *packages dry yeast*
> 3 *tablespoons sugar*
> 1 *tablespoon salt*
> ¼ *cup soft margarine*
> 1 *large egg and 1 egg yolk, well beaten*
> 6 *to* 6½ *cups flour*

Warm bowl, add lukewarm water, sprinkle the yeast over it. Add the sugar, stir until dissolved. Add salt, soft margarine (it may be partially melted), then well-beaten egg and yolk. Stir in 2 cups of flour, mix until smooth. Beat in 1 more cup of flour.

Gradually mix in remainder of the flour until the dough forms a smooth ball beginning to leave the sides of the bowl. Flour hands and knead until smooth and satiny.

Grease a bowl and place dough in it. Let rise until doubled in bulk. Punch down. Grease two 9 x 5″ loaf pans and put dough in them. Let rise again until doubled in bulk.

Preheat oven to 375°.

Bake 35 minutes. Remove, butter tops, cover with linen cloth and let cool on a rack.

GRANDMOTHER'S ROLLS

It occurs to me that the small household has perpetrated a large tragedy—the rarity of the homemade roll. Regular features at the dinner table, without them Sunday breakfasts were a failure.

You can get around the problem of making a minimum quantity of 24 rolls. First, depend on this—everyone will eat at least 2. That takes care of quite a bit.

Plan it this way. Make your dough for dinner rolls the first day. Put the remainder in the refrigerator before it has risen the second time. Butter the top, cover with waxed paper and let it stay until ready to make out another batch.

Before you go to bed, make out a pan, butter the tops, cover with waxed paper and stick back in the refrigerator. Next morning, when you put on the coffee, turn the oven on to warm, put the rolls on top, uncovered, and allow to rise.

You may reheat them in the top of a double boiler or in a bunwarmer. You may double the recipe if you wish.

For 24 rolls.

⅜ *cup shortening*
¼ *cup sugar*
1½ *teaspoons salt*
¾ *cup boiling water*
¼ *cup milk*
1 *beaten egg*
1 *package dry yeast or 1 cake dissolved in* ¼ *cup water*
4 *cups flour*
butter

Preheat oven to 400°.

Put shortening in a large mixing bowl, combine sugar and salt and add. Pour the boiling water over the mixture, dissolving all ingredients. Allow to cool until lukewarm.

Add milk, beaten egg and dissolved yeast with 2 cups of the flour. Mix and beat well with a wooden spoon until smooth.

Add 1½ more cups of the flour until you have a soft dough, mixing well. Turn it out on a lightly floured board and knead until smooth and satiny, adding a little more of the remaining flour as you go along to keep the dough from becoming sticky. This will take about 10 to 15 minutes.

Put the dough into a greased bowl, butter the top and let rise until double in bulk in a warm, non-drafty spot.

If you have time, punch it down and let it rise again.

Make out your rolls, see 3 methods below, place in a greased pan and allow to rise until doubled in bulk again.

Bake rolls in hot (400°) oven for 15 minutes. Serve hot.

METHODS FOR DIFFERENT KINDS OF ROLLS

1. *Regular rolls:* Use a square or rectangular pan and grease. Pinch off enough dough to make a ball about the size of a golf ball. Place in a pan close enough so that they will touch and fuse when risen to double their size.

2. *Cloverleaf rolls:* Use a muffin tin, and grease cups well. Pinch off enough dough to make a little ball about the size of a cherry and place 3 in each cup. They should almost touch as they will fuse when risen to double their bulk. Bake only 12 minutes.

3. *Parkerhouse rolls:* Use a cookie sheet and grease well. Roll out the dough on a floured board. Cut into rounds about 2½″. Butter them. Fold the top half of the round over the bottom so it reaches about ¼″ from the edge. Place them on the sheet far enough apart so they do not touch when risen. Bake only 12 minutes.

SWEET POTATO BREAD

A heavenly color as well as a heavenly flavor. Serve it as you would a regular bread. It is even good for sandwiches.

1 *cup mashed, seasoned sweet potatoes*
1 *cup lukewarm water*
1 *package dry yeast*
1½ *tablespoons sugar*
½ *teaspoon salt*
⅛ *cup softened margarine*
1 *well-beaten egg*
4 *cups flour*

Bake and mash sweet potatoes, seasoning very lightly with salt and sugar.

Warm a large bowl, add the lukewarm water, sprinkle the yeast over it. Add the sugar, stir until dissolved. Add salt, softened margarine, then the well-beaten egg, mixing well. Add 2 cups of flour, mix until smooth. Beat in the mashed sweet potatoes plus 1 more cup of the flour. Gradually knead in the remainder of the flour until the dough forms a smooth ball beginning to leave the sides of the bowl.

Grease a bowl and place dough in it, letting rise until double in bulk. Grease a 9 x 5″ loaf pan and place dough in it, letting rise again until doubled.

Preheat oven to 375°. Bake 35 minutes. Remove, butter top, cover and cool on a rack.

BANANA BREAD

A good in-between bread, serve it with a light meal, for tea or toasted for breakfast. It freezes well, as do most breads.

> ½ *cup vegetable shortening*
> 1 *cup sugar*
> 2 *eggs*
> 1 *cup mashed bananas*
> 2 *cups flour*
> 1 *teaspoon baking powder*
> ½ *teaspoon soda*
> 1 *teaspoon salt*
> ½ *cup chopped nuts*

Preheat oven to 350°.

Cream shortening and sugar, beat in eggs one at a time. Mix bananas in thoroughly. Sift dry ingredients together and blend in. Fold in nuts. Pour into greased 9 x 5″ pan. Push the batter into the corners leaving the center slightly hollowed.

Allow to stand 20 minutes before baking in the moderate (350°) oven for 60 to 70 minutes. Cool on a rack before slicing.

SNOW'S GRAHAM NUT BREAD

A good, sturdy dark bread with a rather subtle, nutty quality. We like it hot, then toasted with butter.

> 2 *scant cups graham flour*
> 1 *scant cup white flour*
> ¾ *teaspoon salt*
> ½ *cup sugar*
> 1½ *cups milk*
> ½ *scant cup dark molasses*
> 1 *rounded teaspoon soda, dissolved in a tiny bit of hot water*
> 1 *cup chopped nuts—preferably walnuts*

Preheat oven to 350°.

Sift flours, salt and sugar together. Add the milk to the molasses, mix well and combine with dry ingredients. Stir in the dissolved soda. Add the chopped nuts.

Grease a loaf pan or a flat baking pan and pour batter in. Bake in the moderate (350°) oven for approximately 50 minutes on until done. It will leave the sides of the pan. Cool on a rack.

AUNT CRETIA'S ROLLED OATS BREAD

Aunt Cretia (called Cretee) was my husband's great, great-aunt Lucretia Guilford. She died when he was a little boy but left fond memories of far more than this sturdy bread.

When people died in old New England, their effects were often auctioned off to settle the estate. Everyone in the family, as well as from the surrounding villages, went as these were gay, all-day outings that provided a good excuse for visiting around.

Sharp-eyed old Aunt Cretia had settled herself in at a distant relative's auction some fifty years ago when she spotted a little candlestand going on the block.

"Why, my sakes," she said, "that belonged to Frances Snow's great-grandmother!" and promptly bid it in, sending it home to

Frances where it belonged. Someone had painted it first green, then barn red. Today, its lovely tawny golden brown applewood is a soft pleasure to us.

Her bread is especially good toasted. Makes three 3 x 6½″ loaves.

2 cups water
1 cup rolled oats
2 tablespoons shortening
1 teaspoon salt
½ cup dark molasses
1 package yeast, dissolved
4–5 cups flour
1 cup ground nuts (optional)

Boil water and pour over the oats, letting stand until lukewarm. Soften shortening. Add it with the salt and molasses, mixing well. Add dissolved yeast, mix again. Beat in 3 to 4 cups of flour and knead, adding additional flour as necessary.

If using the nuts, add with flour prior to kneading stage. Let rise until doubled in bulk, then grease loaf pans and put dough in them. Let rise again until doubled in bulk.

Preheat oven to 350°.

Bake about 30 minutes or until done. Remove from pans, butter tops, cover and cool on a rack.

JEAN SNOW'S DATE NUT BREAD

A crunchy, nutty bread which can be used for tea or even for dessert. We like it sliced off and toasted, as with most of these heavier, old-fashioned breads.

1 cup dates
½ cup sugar
¼ cup butter
¾ cup boiling water
1¾ cups flour
½ teaspoon salt
1 teaspoon soda
1 well-beaten egg
½ cup chopped nuts

Preheat oven to 350°.

Chop dates fine and mix with the sugar. Melt the butter in the boiling water and mix with the dates.

Sift dry ingredients together.

Beat egg well and mix with the dates. Add the dry ingredients and mix thoroughly. Add chopped nuts, mix again.

Grease an 8 x 8″ square pan and pour batter in. Bake in a moderate (350°) oven for 50 minutes or until done. It will leave the sides of the pan.

BOSTON BROWN BREAD

The old Snow version of this famous bread is delicate and relatively light.

1½ cups waterground cornmeal	2 cups milk
1½ cups rye flour	1 well-beaten egg
1 teaspoon soda	½ cup dark molasses
½ teaspoon salt	1 cup raisins (optional)

Sift the dry ingredients together. Stir the milk and beaten egg into the molasses. Combine all ingredients and mix well. Add raisins if desired.

Butter two 1½-quart molds well. If you have no molds, use two 1-pound coffee tins, making tight lids for them out of foil which you tie securely so no steam escapes. Pour batter into molds, filling not more than ¾ full to allow for rising. Cover tightly.

Use a Dutch oven or large kettle and fill with 1″ of water. Cover tightly and bring to a boil. Place molds in it and recover tightly. Steam for 3 hours, checking occasionally to be sure water does not boil away, continuing to add enough to maintain the 1″ level in the kettle.

To serve, let covered molds stand on a rack for about 5 minutes to permit steam to subside, then simply upend molds onto a plate and slice about ¾″ thick while hot. Slice only as much as you will need for a meal and serve with butter. To serve cold, slice the same way. You may freeze this bread tightly wrapped and reheat in foil for about 20 minutes in a moderate (350°) oven, or slice it and toast it.

Delicious with cream cheese and jam, too.

SOFT GINGERBREAD

My husband remembers this from his childhood when his grandmother used to make it. Serve with ice cream or whipped cream.

½ cup dark molasses
½ cup brown sugar
¼ cup lard
¼ cup butter
1 teaspoon ginger
1 teaspoon soda dissolved in ½ cup cold water
½ teaspoon salt
2 cups flour

Preheat oven to 350°.

Combine molasses, sugar, lard, butter and ginger in a heavy saucepan and simmer together 5 minutes. Cool. It will be a candy-like mass. Dissolve the soda in the water and beat in well. Sift flour and salt together. Mix into the molasses thoroughly.

Grease and flour an 8 x 8 x 2″ baking pan and pour batter in. Bake in the moderate (350°) oven for 45 minutes, or until done. Test with a cake tester for doneness.

PORK CAKE

While all of these recipes are unique as far as I know, many are our methods of making well-known dishes. This little concoction, however, was the most baffling of all the old, forgotten recipes, and, as with most of the Snow recipes, there were no instructions and no one to ask.

I didn't even know what it was supposed to look like. And when I asked one of our most famed cooking authorities if he'd heard of such, he said, "Pork pie, yes, pork cake, no."

My mother vaguely remembered having some many years ago as did her sister, although one said with a caramel icing and the other with a white. Both said, "Delicious." I had about given up when, digging around at my aunt's one day, I uncovered something similar, vintage 1900. Emboldened, I reconstructed Grandmother Clary's aberration.

I rather suspect it is different from those my family recalls, as it is more of a bread than the true cake we know today. Try it toasted with butter. All my guinea-pig friends love it.

4 cups flour	*½ cup dark molasses*
1 teaspoon soda	*1½ cups brown sugar*
1 teaspoon cinnamon	*1 cup raisins*
1 teaspoon nutmeg	
1 cup ground pork shoulder with fat (about ½ pound)	
1 cup hot sweet milk	

Preheat oven to 325°.

Sift flour, soda, cinnamon and nutmeg together. Combine ground pork and milk, then add molasses and sugar. Combine all ingredients and beat for 5 minutes, adding raisins for the last minute.

Grease and flour a 9″ square cake pan and fill with batter. Bake in the moderate oven (325°) 1 hour and 15 minutes.

BUTTERMILK BISCUITS

The secret of these tender, flaky biscuits, which are an old Southern staple, is in the kneading. The dough must be lightly pressed, folded over, pressed again, and this procedure followed three or four times. They should be served at once.

Makes about 18 biscuits.

> 2 *cups flour*
> 1 *teaspoon salt*
> 2 *teaspoons baking powder*
> ½ *teaspoon soda*
> 5 *tablespoons shortening*
> 1 *cup buttermilk*

Preheat oven to 450°.

Sift dry ingredients together, cut in shortening with pastry blender or two knives until crumbly like coarse cornmeal. Add buttermilk, pouring into the center of the flour mixture. Stir quickly with a fork until dough leaves the sides of the bowl, about ½ minute. Place dough on a floured board and knead quickly about 3 or 4 times until no lumps appear. Press out with your fingertips or roll out until about ¾ inch thick. Cut with a biscuit cutter. Put on an ungreased baking sheet and bake in a hot (425–450°) oven for about 10 minutes.

MARYLAND BEATEN BISCUITS

Mother relates that her grandmother, Mom Bradley, loved making these so much that the mere mention would send her racing off to the kitchen. And, indeed, they are a labor of love.

Makes about 80 biscuits.

> 5 *cups flour*
> 1½ *teaspoons salt*
> 1 *teaspoon sugar (optional)*
> ½ *cup lard*
> 1¼ *cups water*

Preheat oven to 400°.

Sift flour and salt together, and sugar if used. Cut in the lard until mixture is crumbly with the consistency of coarse cornmeal. Gradually add water, mixing with fingertips. Dough will be very stiff.

Knead it as much as you can. Then place it on a floured board and beat with a wooden mallet or rolling pin until it blisters and cracks, folding the dough every few minutes. It will literally seem to pop. This will take some 20 to 30 minutes and is excellent exercise for the arm muscles.

Form into balls about the size of a small egg and place on a greased cookie sheet. Prick each one in the middle with a fork in an X (they used to have tiny mallets for this) and bake in a hot (400–425°) oven for about 20 minutes.

They should crack at the edges like a cracker when they are done, and be light and even-grained.

SWEET POTATO BISCUITS

A delicate orangey color, an unusual texture and flavor, these are well worth plotting leftover sweet potatoes for.
Makes about 20 to 25 biscuits.

> 1½ *cups flour*
> ¾ *teaspoon salt*
> 2 *tablespoons baking powder*
> ½ *cup shortening*
> ½ *cup cooked, mashed sweet potato*
> 1 *tablespoon sugar*
> ⅔ *cup milk*

Preheat oven to 425°.

Sift flour, salt and baking powder together. Cut in the shortening with a pastry blender or two knives until you have a crumbly mixture.

Mix the cooked, mashed sweet potato with the sugar and the milk. Add to the dry mixture and stir quickly.

Lightly flour a board and roll out about ½″ thick. Cut with a biscuit cutter. Grease a cookie sheet and place on it.

Bake in the hot (425°) oven for 12 to 15 minutes.

OUR MUFFINS—PLAIN, BLUEBERRY AND RAISIN

This makes about 16 muffins.

PLAIN MUFFINS
3 *tablespoons melted margarine*
8 *pats margarine*
2 *beaten eggs*
1 *cup milk*
2 *cups flour*
¾ *teaspoon salt*
1 *tablespoon sugar*
4 *teaspoons baking powder*

Preheat oven to 400°.

Melt the 3 tablespoons of margarine and have sizzling hot, but do not let it burn. At the same time, put about ½ pat of margarine in each section of the muffin tin, so that you can stick tin in the oven to melt the margarine while you're mixing the muffins. You want to coat each section before pouring the batter in.

Beat eggs until light and add the milk. Sift flour, salt, sugar and baking powder together.

Add the dry ingredients to the liquid and beat only until well blended. Pour the hot melted margarine into the batter and stir. Then pour the batter into the greased tin, filling each section ⅔ full.

Bake in the hot (400°) oven about 18 to 20 minutes.

BLUEBERRY MUFFINS

Dredge ½ cup of blueberries with ¼ cup of the flour and quickly mix them in after all ingredients are blended. Proceed as above.

RAISIN MUFFINS

Proceed exactly as with blueberry muffins, but substitute raisins.

CORNMEAL MUFFINS

This makes about 16 muffins.

>   3 *tablespoons melted margarine*
>   2 *beaten eggs*
>   1 *cup milk*
>   1 *cup flour*
>   1 *cup waterground cornmeal*
>   ¾ *teaspoon salt*
>   4 *teaspoons baking powder*
>   *bacon fat or additional margarine*

Preheat oven to 400°.

Melt the margarine and have hot. Beat eggs, add milk and melted fat. Sift the flour, cornmeal, salt and baking powder together.

Melt enough bacon fat or margarine in the muffin tins so each is coated with a bit of residue on the bottom.

Add the dry ingredients to the milk mixture, blending thoroughly. Pour into the greased tins, filling about ⅔ full. Bake in hot (400°) oven until brown, about 18 to 20 minutes.

Serve at once with butter and marmalade or jam.

OUR RAISED MUFFINS

Very light and delicious, these take a bit more time and effort than regular plain muffins but are well worth both. Serve them for small luncheon parties as well as any time the mood strikes.

Makes 18 muffins.

>   1 *package dry yeast*   ¼ *cup sugar*
>   ¼ *cup lukewarm water*   3 *tablespoons margarine*
>   1 *cup warm milk*   1 *beaten egg*
>   1¾ *teaspoons salt*   3½ *cups sifted flour*

Dissolve yeast in lukewarm water. Heat milk until tiny bubbles appear around the edge. Do *not* boil. Add salt, sugar and margarine to milk and mix, then allow to cool until lukewarm.

Combine yeast and milk mixtures, beaten egg, then add ½ of the flour, beating until smooth using a wooden spoon. Add the remainder of the flour and beat again until smooth and light. Cover and let rise until double in bulk.

Beat dough again. Grease muffin tins and fill ⅔ full. Cover and let rise again until double in bulk.

Preheat oven to 375°. Bake on middle rack about 20 minutes or until brown and done. Serve hot.

WHOLE WHEAT POPOVERS

Temperamental little creatures, these, so don't be upset if you have a bit of trouble the first time. They're worth it.

Makes about 9 popovers.

⅔ *cup white flour*
¼ *teaspoon salt*
⅓ *cup whole wheat flour*
2 *beaten eggs*
1 *cup milk*
1 *tablespoon melted shortening*

Preheat oven to 450°. Grease pan.

Sift white flour and salt together. Add whole wheat flour and resift. Combine beaten eggs and milk, then add melted shortening. Mix into the dry ingredients; beat well with a rotary beater.

Have well-greased popover or muffin tin ready and pour the batter into it at once filling sections ¾ full. Bake in the very hot (450°) oven for 25 minutes. Do not open oven, but reduce temperature to 350° and bake 12 minutes longer.

Remove one to test. If not quite done, it will collapse. By this time, the others are sure to be done. Each oven is different, so you may have to adjust your timing accordingly.

Serve at once.

AUNT JANIE REVELL'S RICE PONE

The original of this says, "It's better than good." A very, very old recipe that has been used in the family for well over a hundred years. Rice pone is not really a bread-bread, but, as with spoon-bread, is soft. It has a custardy consistency. When cold, slice it and fry in butter or toast it in the broiler and butter it. Heavenly good.

The rice should be soft. Originally, it was cooked in milk in the top of a double-boiler. Try cooking your rice in milk or half milk and half water.

For 10 people.

>   2 *cups cooked rice*
>   2 *cups cornmeal*
>   1 *tablespoon baking powder*
>   ½ *teaspoon salt (or more to taste)*
>   ¼ *cup sugar*
>   1 *tablespoon lard*
>   1 *quart milk*
>   5 *eggs*

Preheat oven to 350°.

Cook rice in well-salted water or milk or half and half. Beat well with the cornmeal. Add baking powder, salt and sugar, mixing well. Melt lard. Mix well with dry ingredients, then add milk, mixing again. Separate and beat eggs. When yolks are creamy, mix into batter. When whites are stiff, fold them in gently.

Grease two 9 x 5 x 3″ loaf pans or use one large 3-quart casserole and pour in batter. Bake in the moderate (350°) oven 30 to 40 minutes. Test with a silver knife at 30 minutes. It it comes out clean, they are done.

If you are using leftover rice, be sure to check for salt.

FRITTERS—FRUIT AND VEGETABLE

Good critters at breakfast, lunch or dinner. Made with squashes or corn, they look and act more like griddlecakes and can be served as a luncheon entree or a dinner vegetable. Try them with crisp bacon and maple syrup. Made with fruits, they are on the sweet side. Apple fritters make good friends with sausage for breakfast or a pork roast for dinner. All fruit fritters are delicious desserts.

APPLE, PEACH OR BANANA FRITTERS

For 6 people.

THE BATTER

1 *cup flour*
¼ *teaspoon salt*
2 *teaspoons baking powder*
2 *tablespoons sugar*

1 *well-beaten egg*
¾ *cup milk (scant)*
cooking oil

Sift dry ingredients together. Beat egg well and add the milk to it. Mix in dry ingredients as quickly as possible to get a smooth batter. It must be thick enough to coat the fruit without being pasty, but should not be too runny. Add milk or flour to correct thickness, if necessary. Set aside.

THE FRUIT

Peel, core and slice apples into quarters. Peel peaches and halve, removing pit. Peel bananas and halve, then slice halves down the middle. Pieces should be large enough to permit handling with a fork.

You may sprinkle the peaches and bananas with sugar and let stand a bit to sweeten them up, if desired.

TO COOK

You may fry in deep fat, or in a heavy skillet on top of the stove using about ½″ of fat. Either way, have fat sizzling hot.

Dip fruit into batter and coat thoroughly, letting excess drip off. Then fry until golden brown, turning once, if using the skillet method. Drain on paper towel or brown paper, sprinkle with powdered sugar and serve at once. Be careful not to let your fat cool off before you put in the second batch.

SQUASH FRITTERS

For 4 people.

> 3 tablespoons flour
> ½ teaspoon salt
> 1 teaspoon baking powder
> 1 cup seasoned, cooked mashed squash
> 1 beaten egg or 2 beaten egg yolks
> ⅓ cup milk
> 3 tablespoons butter

Mix flour, salt and baking powder together. In a separate bowl mix the mashed squash and beaten egg, then add milk. Add dry ingredients, blending gently. Melt butter on griddle and pour 2 tablespoons into the batter, leaving the remaining butter on the griddle. Have griddle hot, but not sizzling. Drop batter by spoonfuls onto the griddle and fry as you would griddlecakes, until browned, turning once. Drain on paper towel or brown paper.

CORN FRITTERS

For 6 people.

> 1 cup flour
> ½ teaspoon salt
> 2 teaspoons baking powder
> 1 teaspoon sugar
> ⅔ to 1 cup milk
> 2 well-beaten eggs
> 1 cup whole kernel corn, canned or leftover fresh
> 3 tablespoons butter

Sift flour, salt, baking powder and sugar together. Mix milk and eggs. Blend with the dry ingredients, stir corn in lightly. Batter should be thin, so add milk if necessary. Melt the butter on the griddle and pour 2 tablespoons into the batter, leaving the remaining fat on the griddle. Proceed as with squash fritters.

GRANDMOTHER CLARY'S CORNMEAL GRIDDLE CAKES WITH MAPLE SYRUP

Grandmother Clary, my husband's grandmother, was a strong-minded New England teetotaler who worked for women's suffrage and the temperance party. She was the first woman to run for public office in the state of Massachusetts, long before women had the vote. Naturally, she ran on the prohibition ticket. She was ridiculed and, indeed, vilified, but managed to pull a surprising number of votes.

When she wasn't running, here is how she made griddle cakes.

Makes a dozen cakes—for 4 people.

1 *tablespoon cornmeal*
1½ *cups flour*
2 *heaping teaspoons baking powder*
1 *teaspoon salt*
¾ *cup milk*
¾ *cup cream*

Sift all dry ingredients together. Mix with milk and cream. Batter should be lumpy but thin. If it seems too thick, add more milk. Pour in large spoonfuls on hot, slightly greased griddle, cooking until bubbly in center. Turn quickly and cook only until golden brown.

Serve at once with butter and maple syrup.

MEMORIES OF SNOW FARM MAPLE SYRUP

A griddle cake without maple syrup is like spring without a jonquil! At Snow Farm, however, maple syrup was more than a topping for a griddle cake, it was a business for at least a century.

Late in February when the hoarfrost still curtained the windows and the logs burned steadily in the high, shallow fireplaces, the sugaring season began. The oxen, their coats riffling in the chill winds, were hitched to the big woodshod sled, laden with sap buckets. They labored up the sugaring roads that honeycombed the mountain, getting as far into the sugar orchard as possible.

The men then sloughed through the deep snow to bore holes into the sugar maples for little sap spigots, each with a hook to hang the wooden sap bucket on. A mighty maple might take as many as 6 spigots, dripping enough sap to fill the buckets every 24 hours.

Then began the drudgery of gathering, for the rounds had to be made daily. The sled was loaded with the gathering tub. The men, weighted with sap yokes across their shoulders to carry big pails, trudged slowly through the orchard, emptying 6 buckets into each pail, then picking their way back to the sled. It took some 32 gallons of sap just to make one gallon of syrup. So it went, over and over and over again, hour after hour, day after day until the first budding of the trees when the sap turned bitter and milky, as if the trees were saying to man, "Enough. I have given you all I can spare. Now my sap is needed for myself."

When the spigots were removed, the trees quickly healed their wounds, covering them with new bark that in a year or so gave no testimony to man's assault.

Meanwhile, back in the fall, the sugarhouse had been stacked to its eaves with logs. As the sap began to pour into the vat, the fires had to be continually stoked, burning day and night to boil the sap down until it was ready to be drawn off and canned as syrup.

Part of the new syrup was boiled down again until it became much thicker. It was then beaten with enormous wooden paddles as it cooled. This process was done in two stages: thick, to make "soft sugar" which was spread on bread like jam; thicker, to make maple sugar candy.

The boys made a quick sweet by taking the thickened syrup before it was beaten, then mixing it with snow to form a wonderful, waxy kind of chewy candy.

Just a few years ago, we had the last can of the last batch of syrup from the Snow sugar orchards, poured sadly over a stack of griddle cakes.

CORNMEAL GRIDDLE CAKES— SOUTHERN MARYLAND STYLE

Makes about a dozen small cakes—for 3 or 4 people.

> 2 *beaten eggs*
> 1½ *cups milk*
> 1½ *cups flour*
> 1½ *cups cornmeal*
> 1 *teaspoon salt*
> 2 *teaspoons baking powder*
> 4 *tablespoons melted bacon fat or butter*

Beat eggs, add milk. Sift dry ingredients together and stir into egg mixture until just blended. Batter will be a bit lumpy. Add melted fat. (If batter seems thick, add milk, as it should be thin.) Cook on hot, greased griddle, turning once.

Serve with bacon, melted butter and hot maple syrup.

BREADCRUMB GRIDDLE CAKES

There are no griddle cakes as light and tender as these. They are the ultimate, as well as being a good way to take care of stale bread.

Makes about a dozen small cakes—for 3 or 4 people.

  1½ *cups breadcrumbs*
  1½ *cups milk*
  2 *tablespoons butter*
  ½ *cup flour*
  ½ *teaspoon salt*
  4 *teaspoons baking powder*
  2 *beaten eggs*

Use light, white bread and tear into tiny pieces. Scald milk, adding butter to melt. Mix with breadcrumbs and let mixture sit overnight.

Sift dry ingredients together. Beat eggs well. Add both to the breadcrumb mixture, stirring gently.

Have griddle hot, using melted butter or bacon grease. Put large spoonfuls of batter on the griddle, cooking until bubbly in the center. Turn carefully as these are very tender and need only a few seconds on each side.

Serve with butter, syrup or honey.

RICE GRIDDLE CAKES

Makes about 16 small cakes—for 4 to 6 people.

  1 *cup flour*
  ½ *teaspoon salt*
  ½ *teaspoon sugar*
  1 *teaspoon baking powder*
  1 *cup cooked, salted rice*
  1 *beaten egg yolk*
  1 *cup milk*
  1 *stiffly beaten egg white*

Sift dry ingredients together. Be sure your rice is fluffy, not mushy, and stir in. Mix beaten egg yolk with the milk and combine with the flour and rice mixture. Fold in the egg white. Cook on a hot, greased griddle as you would any griddle cakes.

I cook a tiny one first to check for the amount of salt, as you may wish to add a bit more depending on how salty the rice is.

Serve at once with butter, syrup or jam.

CHEESE WAFERS

Serve these with cocktails or with soups. They'll simply melt away.

Makes about 60 wafers.

> 1 *pound grated sharp cheese*
> 1 *pound butter*
> 4 *cups flour*
> ¼ *teaspoon baking powder*
> *salt and red pepper to taste*

Grate cheese. Cream butter and cheese together. Sift flour and baking powder together and mix in. Add salt and the red pepper to taste. Dough will be a stiff, cookie-type. Make rolls about 1½ to 2″ in diameter, wrap well and chill.

When ready to bake, preheat oven to 350°.

Grease cookie sheet. Slice rolls of dough very thin and place on cookie sheet as for cookies. Bake until tanned, about 10 minutes.

Serve hot or cold.

STUFFINGS

BREAD STUFFING

This is light and delicious and doesn't wind up a soggy mass. It is basically the same for chicken, turkey or fish. Avoid heavy breads for this.

FOR CHICKEN—3 POUNDS
5 *slices buttered, dry white bread*
1 *tablespoon minced green pepper*
3 to 4 *sprigs chopped parsley*
1 *small chopped onion*
¼ *teaspoon thyme*
2 or 3 *crumbled basil leaves*
1 *stalk chopped celery*
dash of marjoram
¼ *teaspoon salt*
dash of black pepper
¼ *cup melted butter*
1 *tablespoon water*
1 *cup fluffed raisins*

Butter the dry bread and toast it, crumbling fine while still warm. It should be in very small pieces, not powdery. Prepare the other ingredients and mix with the bread. Add the melted butter and toss. Add a little of the water, until stuffing is just moist, continuing to add if necessary. Taste and correct for salt and pepper.

Fluff raisins by putting in boiling water for 5 minutes. Add to dressing by tossing in.

FOR TURKEY—12 POUNDS

Use 1 loaf of bread and increase all other ingredients three-fold.

FOR FISH OR SHRIMP—3- TO 4-POUND FISH

You will have to judge for the number of shrimp you wish to stuff. For the fish, use 3 to 4 slices of bread and decrease other amounts slightly.

Omit marjoram and raisins.

OYSTER STUFFING

This is a refreshing change, particularly with turkey. I like to stuff half the turkey with regular bread dressing and half with oyster dressing.

Follow the recipe for bread stuffing and omit the raisins. If your oysters are large, cut them in half.

FOR CHICKEN—3 POUNDS

Use about 6 oysters.

FOR TURKEY—12 POUNDS

Use about 1½ pints of oysters.

CRAB STUFFING

The ultimate stuffing for fish or jumbo shrimp, this is made essentially like the crab cake. For a 4- to 5-pound fish or about 3 dozen shrimp.

1 *pound regular or special crab*
2 *slices dry white bread*
⅛ *teaspoon red pepper*
1 *tablespoon chopped green pepper*
1 *tablespoon finely chopped parsley*
1 *teaspoon dry mustard*
⅛ *teaspoon salt*
2 *slightly beaten eggs*
½ *cup milk*
¼ *cup melted butter*

Pick crab carefully. Crumble bread powder-fine. Toss red and green pepper, parsley, mustard and salt with the crumbs. Combine the slightly beaten eggs with the milk. Add the crumb mixture to it and toss lightly. Add crab, toss again. Correct seasonings. Add melted butter, toss once more.

Stuff lightly into the fish or shrimp and proceed with individual recipe.

PICKLES AND CONSERVES

ANN SANDS' PICKLING INSTRUCTIONS—1835

Do not keep pickles in common earthen-ware, as the glazing contains lead, and combines with the vinegar. Vinegar for pickling should be sharp, though not the sharpest kind, as it injures the pickles. If you use copper, bell-metal, or brass vessels, for pickling, never allow the vinegar to cool in them, as it is then poisonous. Add a teaspoonful of alum and a teacup of salt to each three gallons of vinegar, and tie up a bag with pepper, ginger-root, spices of all the different sorts in it, and you have vinegar prepared for any pickling.

Keep pickles only in wood or stone-ware. Anything that has held grease will spoil pickles. Stir pickles occasionally, and if there are any soft ones take them out and scald the vinegar, and pour it hot over the pickles. Keep enough vinegar to cover them well. If it is weak, take fresh vinegar and pour on hot. Do not boil vinegar or spice above five minutes.

GRANDMOTHER'S MUSTARD PICKLES

Variations of this pickle seem to exist all over, but these are the best I ever tasted. Try them on broccoli or cabbage for a new taste treat.

Makes about 12 to 14 pints.

24 medium cucumbers
4 cups small white onions
2 heads cauliflower
8 cups small, hard green tomatoes
6 green peppers
3 red peppers
1 small bunch celery
1 cup salt
1 gallon water
3 cups sugar
4 teaspoons celery seed
8 teaspoons powdered mustard
¾ cup flour
1 tablespoon turmeric
3 quarts vinegar
1 pint jar gherkins (small or cut up)

If cucumbers are young and tender, simply wash and dice. If not, they will have to be peeled. Peel onions. Break cauliflower into flowerets. Stem tomatoes, leave whole. Chop peppers. Chop celery. Mix salt with water, add vegetables and soak overnight. Scald in the brine and drain well.

Mix all dry ingredients with vinegar to make a thick paste, then cook in a double boiler until thick. Pour over the hot drained vegetables. Cut up gherkins and add. Pack in hot sterilized jars with glass or plastic lids. Process in boiling water bath for 15 minutes.

BREAD AND BUTTER PICKLES

Nobody seems to know why these are so named. I figure it's because they go with everything just like bread and butter. There were always jars lined up in grandmother's pantry. Her favorite recipe came through her mother's cousin Betty Culver, on the Eastern Shore.

This will make 10 pints.

> 16 *cups cucumbers (about 5½ pounds)*
> 8 *small white onions*
> 3 *green peppers*
> ½ *cup salt*
> 1 *quart ice*
> 5 *cups sugar (white or brown)*
> 1½ *teaspoons turmeric*
> ½ *teaspoon ground cloves*
> 2 *tablespoons mustard seed*
> 1 *teaspoon celery seed*
> 5 *cups cider vinegar*

Select crisp, fresh cucumbers. Wash without peeling, slice very thin crosswise. Shred onions and peppers. Mix together with salt and bury the ice in the mixture, letting stand three hours under a weighted lid to prevent air entering. Drain thoroughly.

Mix sugar, turmeric, cloves, mustard seed, celery seed together well, add vinegar. Pour over drained vegetables, then place over low heat, stirring occasionally with a wooden paddle. Heat until scalding (little bubbles will appear) but do not boil. Seal in hot, sterilized jars with glass or plastic lids. Process in boiling water bath for 15 minutes.

PIN MONEY PICKLES

Another of my grandmother's cousin Betty Culver's Eastern Shore recipes. A good way to use up those tomatoes and cucumbers.

Makes about 10 pints.

> 12 *cups cucumbers (about 4 pounds)*
> 4 *cups green tomatoes (about 1½ pounds)*
> 2 *cups sweet green peppers (about ½ pound)*
> 6 *cups sweet red peppers (about 2 pounds)*

Ingredients continued overleaf

> *2 hot red peppers*
> *2 ounces white mustard seed*
> *1 ounce celery seed*
> *1½ pounds each white and brown sugar*
> *½ gallon vinegar*

Be sure all vegetables are crisp and fresh. Use unwaxed cucumbers and wash without peeling, then slice thin. Chop all other vegetables fine.

Combine all ingredients in a large kettle and cook slowly, covered, until done. They will be firm but should not get gooey.

Seal in hot, sterilized jars with glass or plastic lids. Process in boiling water bath for 15 minutes.

SWEET PICKLE WATERMELON RIND

My Aunt Bong, who rescued great-grandmother's recipe from oblivion years ago, says there are just two important factors to remember: a thick rind and a watchful eye that cooks the rind just enough to make it tender without losing its crispness.

Makes about 8 pints.

> *9 cups watermelon rind*
> *1 quart water*
> *¼ cup salt*
> *5 cups sugar*
> *2 cups cider vinegar*
> *1 cup water*
> *1 tablespoon whole cloves*
> *1 tablespoon whole allspice*
> *1 tablespoon cinnamon or 1 cinnamon stick*
> *lemon and/or orange slices*

Skin rind and cut into ½-inch cubes or equivalent. Soak 12 hours in the quart of water with ¼ cup salt. Drain. Boil 10 minutes in clear water until tender but still crisp. Drain again.

Make syrup by combining sugar, vinegar, the cup of water and spices, and boiling 5 minutes.

Add rind and several slices of fruit and boil 15 minutes until rind is transparent. Seal in hot, sterilized jars with glass or plastic lids.

RIPE TOMATO PICKLE

The old recipe says, "this may be crocked and put in the icebox if to be used soon."

For 2 pints.

> 4 *cups tomatoes (about 1½ pounds)*
> ¾ *cup cider vinegar*
> 2 *sticks cinnamon*
> ½ *piece whole mace*
> 12 *whole cloves*
> 2 *cups sugar*
> ½ *teaspoon salt*

Skin and quarter the tomatoes. Put all ingredients in a kettle and boil slowly until the tomatoes are transparent and the juice has the consistency of 30% cream (it will be fairly thick). Seal in hot, sterilized jars with glass or plastic lids. Process in boiling water bath for 15 minutes.

AUNT FANNY'S PEPPER RELISH

Hot, authoritative, it'll liven up your hamburgers, hot dogs, steaks, whatever. It's rather appropriate that it came down from my great, great-aunt Fanny Phippin, since she was a hot, peppery little wisp of a dame who'd shrunk to a mere 4'10" by the time she was ninety. None of which deterred her from flirting with every attractive man she met.

Makes about 4 pints.

> 2 *cups red peppers*
> 2 *cups green peppers*
> 2 *cups onions*
> 2 *tablespoons salt*
> 1 *cup sugar*
> 2 *cups vinegar*

Stem and seed peppers. Peel onions. Grind together and cover with boiling water. Let stand 15 minutes, then drain. Mix salt, sugar and vinegar. Pour over vegetables, mix well, boil 15 minutes. Seal in hot, sterilized jars with glass or plastic lids. Process in boiling water bath for 15 minutes.

PICCALILLI

In my old book, this was spelled "Pickle lilli," probably its original name.

Makes about 16 pints, enough for all your Christmas presents.

> 32 *cups green tomatoes (about 10½ pounds)*
> 4 *medium-large onions*
> 1 *head cabbage*
> 2 *quarts cider vinegar*
> 4 *cups brown sugar*
> 1 *tablespoon cinnamon*
> 1 *tablespoon mustard seed*
> 1 *tablespoon black pepper*
> 2 *tablespoons salt*
> 1 *heaping teaspoon allspice*
> 1 *heaping teaspoon cloves*

Chop tomatoes, onions and cabbage quite fine. Put all ingredients into a kettle and cook until tender. Seal in hot, sterilized jars with glass or plastic lids. Process in boiling water bath for 15 minutes.

PEPPER HASH

Makes about 6 pints.

12 *green peppers*
12 *red peppers*
12 *onions*
1 *head celery cabbage*
3 *pints vinegar*
2 *cups sugar*
3 *tablespoons salt*
¼ *teaspoon dry mustard*

Seed, stem and chop peppers fine. Cover with boiling water and let stand 5 minutes. Drain.

Chop onions and celery cabbage. You should have as much cabbage as you do peppers. Add to the peppers and pour boiling water over them. Let stand another 5 minutes. Drain.

Put vinegar with remaining ingredients in a large kettle, add the vegetables and bring to a boil, cover and cook only until vegetables are just tender.

Seal in hot, sterilized jars with glass or plastic lids. Process in boiling water bath for 15 minutes.

CHILI SAUCE

Mom Bradley, my great-grandmother, was a lusty, laughing, much-adored woman with dark grey eyes glinting behind steel-rimmed glasses that rode solidly in the crevice they'd eroded over the bridge of her nose. Her grey hair was thin and constantly straying from its scanty knot.

Over her 80-some years she had grown a prodigious number of warts and moles which always held a strange, rather fearful fascination for me as a child, secretly wondering if they were catching.

She was a great storyteller. One of my favorites was about the ball of lightning.

"We were just sitting in the parlor one summer day," she said, "with the thunder cracking around the house in a fearful manner. Suddenly, we saw a ball of lightning roll right up the front walk, bounce up the steps, slither across the veranda and through the door into the hall. It started to go upstairs, then changed its mind and came right into the parlor at my feet. It just kept right on going through the parlor door back out to the veranda, down the steps and out the walk."

This was her recipe and her mother's.

Makes about 8 pints.

> 36 *ripe tomatoes*
> 6 *large green peppers*
> 8 *medium onions*
> 4 *tablespoons salt*
> ¾ *cup brown sugar*
> ¾ *cup white sugar*
> 4 *tablespoons mustard seed*
> 4 *tablespoons celery seed*
> 1 *hot red pepper, chopped fine*
> 1 *teaspoon allspice*
> 1 *teaspoon whole cloves*
> 1 *teaspoon cinnamon*
> 1 *pint vinegar*
> *few leaves fresh basil*

Grind tomatoes, peppers and onions together coarsely. Add all other ingredients except the basil. Boil slowly, covered, until thick, approximately 4 hours.

Crumble the basil leaves in. Seal in hot, sterilized jars.

RHUBARB RELISH

An ancient recipe that came originally from Dedham, this makes 4 pints.

2 *pounds rhubarb*
1 *pint vinegar*
2 *pounds onions*
2 *pounds brown sugar*
1 *teaspoon salt*
1 *teaspoon pepper*
cinnamon
cloves
celery salt

Dice rhubarb and cook with vinegar for 20 minutes. Chop onions fine and add with sugar, salt and pepper. Add cinnamon, cloves and celery salt to taste. Cook slowly for 1 hour. Seal in hot, sterilized jars with glass or plastic lids. Process in boiling water bath for 15 minutes.

FRANCES SNOW'S YELLOW TOMATO CONSERVE

You'll find versions of these served in New England inns with cottage cheese and other condiments as a first course, as well as an accompaniment to the meal. These are great, just as they made them on Snow Farm.

Makes about 8 pints.

4 *pounds yellow tomatoes*
1 *lemon*
8 *cups sugar*
½ *pound candied chopped ginger*
1 *cup water*

Stem and wash tomatoes. Cut lemon in paper-thin slices. Combine all ingredients in a big kettle and cook until thick. Seal in hot, sterilized jars with glass or plastic lids. Process in boiling water bath for 15 minutes.

WHOLE TOMATOES FOR WINTER USE

This is a 19th century Snow Farm recipe, copied herewith in its entirety. I am unable to figure out why the flannel was important, nor has anyone alive been able to enlighten me!

Fill a large stone jar with ripe, and perfectly sound, whole tomatoes, adding a few cloves and a sprinkling of sugar between each layer. Cover well with one-half cold vinegar and one-half water. Place a piece of thick flannel over the jar, letting it fall well down into the vinegar, then tie down with a cover of brown paper. These will keep all winter, and are not harmed even if the flannel collects mould.

CORN RELISH

I can eat this by the bowlful, especially with cottage cheese.

Makes about 5 pints.

18 *large ears corn*
2 *green peppers*
1 *red pepper*
4 *large onions*
1¼ *pounds brown sugar*
¼ *cup salt*
3 *tablespoons celery seed*
3½ *tablespoons dry mustard*
2 *quarts of cider vinegar*

Cut corn off the cob, but don't scrape. Chop peppers and onions fine. Mix all ingredients together and boil slowly 15 to 20 minutes until done. Seal in hot, sterilized jars with glass or plastic lids. Process in boiling water bath for 15 minutes.

CRANBERRY CHUTNEY

This recipe came into legend through Toodie Weeden Brady, my grandfather's "off-cousin"—that is, one whose relationship is a bit cloudy, but who is granted family status anyhow.

Makes about 2 pints.

> 4 cups cranberries
> 2 cups light brown sugar
> 1 cup white raisins
> ½ cup lemon juice
> 1 teaspoon salt
> 2 tablespoons finely chopped onions
> ½ cup chopped pecans (optional)

Wash and drain berries, then grind. Chop the onion fine. Add to ground berries with remainder of ingredients. Add nuts if desired. Mix thoroughly. Refrigerate at least 24 hours before using.

If you make enough at Thanksgiving, you can keep it over through Christmas.

SWEET PICKLED PEACHES, PLUMS OR PEARS

Makes about 7 pints.

> 8 pounds fruit
> 4 pounds brown sugar
> 1 quart cider vinegar
> Spice bag of:
>   2 ounces whole cloves
>   2 ounces stick cinnamon
>   ½ ounce gingerroot (optional)

For peaches: wash and defuzz. For plums: wash and prick skins. For pears: select not quite ripe ones if using Bartletts. Be sure any pears are firm and not overly ripe. Wash and remove the blossom ends.

Boil the sugar in the vinegar with the spice bag until you have a syrup. Pour over the fruit and let stand overnight.

Drain and reboil the syrup for 10 minutes longer. Add the fruit to it and cook uncovered until just tender. Time will depend on the fruit used.

Seal in hot, sterilized jars with glass or plastic lids. Process in boiling water bath for 15 minutes.

SNOW FARM GINGER PEARS

Serve these as a dessert over vanilla ice cream or as a condiment with meats.

Makes about 6 or 7 pints.

> 8 *pounds pears*
> 4 *lemons and grated peel*
> 4 *pounds sugar*
> 1 *cup water*
> ½ *pound chopped sugared ginger*

Select firm, not too ripe pears. Peel, core and quarter or slice them. Grate the lemons, then dig the meat out of the rind, removing seeds and membrane.

Dissolve the sugar in the water. Combine all ingredients including the chopped ginger. Simmer together uncovered until thick, about 3 hours.

Seal in hot, sterilized jars with glass or plastic lids. Process in boiling water bath for 15 minutes.

ANN SANDS' PLUM MARMALADE—1835

To 4 quarts of ripe plums allow two quarts of sugar-house molasses. Put them in a preserving kettle, or in a large earthen jug (which will do as well). Pour the molasses over them. Set them on coals and let them boil slowly all day, frequently renewing the coals and mashing down the plums with a spoon.

When they are done, pour them into a broadpan and set them to cool. Pick out all the stones before you put the plums away in a jar. Tie up the jar with brandy-paper and keep it in a dry place.

This marmalade will keep a year or more, and is very good for pies, always sweetening it with sugar before you use it.

CAPE CARROT MARMALADE

A yummy marmalade, made with those silly carrots that have such chameleon personalities.

Makes approximately 1 pint.

> *2 lemons*
> *2½ cups sliced carrots (about 1 pound)*
> *2 cups sugar*
> *1 cup lemon water*
> *2 tablespoons carrot water*

Cut lemons up and seed. Put into saucepan with about 1½ cups of water, cover and cook until tender, about 30 minutes. Clean and slice carrots. Put into another saucepan with just enough water to cover and cook until tender, about 20–25 minutes.

Drain both, reserving the liquid separately. Put sugar into heavy saucepan, add 1 cup of the water lemons were cooked in and 2 tablespoons of the water carrots were cooked in. Combine carrots and lemons and chop. Add to the sugar water.

Boil as slowly as possible, uncovered, until syrupy. When the mixture is thick enough to separate into drops on a spoon as it is poured, the marmalade is done. Total cooking time will be about 1½ hours.

Seal in hot, sterilized jars.

APPLE BUTTER

Makes about 8 quarts.

> *2 gallons sweet cider*
> *½ bushel (32 pounds) of apples*
> *1 teaspoon cinnamon*
> *1 teaspoon grated nutmeg*
> *1 teaspoon allspice*
> *3 tablespoons lemon juice*
> *grated peel of 2 lemons*

Boil cider down in a large kettle, uncovered, to 1 gallon. Use Greenings, Baldwins or other apples which cook tender quickly. Peel, core and cut into small pieces. Put apples into boiling cider, filling kettle as full as possible, covering tightly.

Cook as many apples at a time as you can get in the kettle, removing them as they are done and refilling the kettle, until all are cooked.

Mash apples very fine and return to the kettle. Add spices and cook very, very slowly, uncovered, stirring often with a wooden spoon or paddle, until thick.

Check the seasonings and correct to the spiciness you desire.

Seal in hot, sterilized jars.

ANN SANDS' POTATO CHEESE—1835

In Thuringia and part of Saxony, a kind of potato cheese is made that is much sought after. The following is the recipe: Select good white potatoes, boil them and when cold, peel and reduce them to a pulp in a rasp or mortar, to five pounds of this pulp, which must be uniform and homogeneous, add a pint of sour milk and the requisite portion of salt; knead the whole well, cover it and let it remain three or four days, according to the season, then knead it afresh, and place the cheese in small baskets, when they will part with their superfluous moisture; dry them in the shade, and place them in layers in large pots or kegs where they remain a fortnight.

The older they are the finer they become. This cheese has the advantage of never engendering worms and of being preserved fresh for many years provided it is kept in a dry place, and in well closed vessels.

SAUCES

HOT LEMON SAUCE

When I was a little girl, I used to beg my grandmother not to forget the hot sauce to go with the hard sauce, for the combination is just out of this world. Try it with plum pudding, fruit puddings, cake with or without the hard sauce.

Makes about 1¼ cups of sauce—for 4 people.

> ½ cup sugar
> 1 tablespoon cornstarch
> 1 cup boiling water
> pinch of salt
> 1½ tablespoons lemon juice, to taste
> 2 tablespoons butter
> grating of nutmeg
> grated peel from 1 lemon

Mix sugar and cornstarch. Add boiling water and salt. Boil mixture until thick and clear. Beat in lemon juice, butter, nutmeg and grated peel. Serve hot. (May be prepared ahead and reheated over hot water.)

BRANDY OR RUM SAUCE
Substitute either for the lemon juice, to taste.

VANILLA SAUCE
Substitute 1 teaspoon vanilla for the lemon juice. Omit peel.

CUSTARD SAUCE

Serve hot or cold over desserts such as Snow pudding, apple dumplings, blackberry roly poly. This is the sauce to use for Tipsy Pudding or any tired cake.

Makes about 2 cups of sauce—for 4 to 6 people.

> 2 cups milk
> 2 beaten egg yolks
> ¼ cup sugar
> pinch of salt
> 1 teaspoon vanilla
> grating of nutmeg (optional)

Scald milk in the top of a double boiler. Beat egg yolks until frothy, then beat the sugar into them. Off heat, pour the hot milk into the egg mixture a little at a time, blending well as you go along. Add salt.

Put the sauce back over simmering water and cook until it thickens enough to coat a spoon, stirring constantly. Add vanilla and nutmeg if used.

HARD SAUCE

The secret of fluffy hard sauce is the boiling water which we add. Make this ahead, shape into a leaf or mold as you wish, after it begins to chill. Makes about 1½ cups.

For 6 to 8 people.

> ½ cup butter
> 1-2 cups sifted powdered sugar
> 1 teaspoon vanilla, brandy or rum
> 1 teaspoon boiling water

Cream butter and sugar until light and fluffy. Add or subtract from the amount of sugar to get the desired consistency. Add vanilla or spirits. Beat in boiling water.

SWEETS

BLACKBERRY ROLY POLY

Heaven is a sunny day in the blackberry patch when every berry is worth two scratches. My grandmother used to make this for me with those rare, juicy gifts from the gods. Serve hot with raw sugar or custard sauce (p. 161), or cold with hot or cold custard. A good way to use leftover rice, too.

For 8 people.

> 1 *cup cold, cooked rice*
> 1 *quart blackberries*
> ¼ *teaspoon salt*
> ½ *teaspoon sugar*
> 2 *gratings nutmeg*
> 1 *teaspoon lemon juice (optional)*
> 18″ *square unbleached muslin*

Cook rice and let it get cold. Cap and wash berries, drain. Mix the salt and sugar together and sprinkle over the berries. Grate nutmeg over them. Add lemon juice if using. Blackberries are very tender, so be gentle.

Spread muslin out and cover to within 2″ of its edges with the rice. Spread the berries over the top. Roll it up like a jelly roll, being sure the muslin is closed all along the length. Tie ends together securely, and tie it around the length a few times too.

Place on a rack in a kettle over (not in) boiling water, cover and steam approximately 25 minutes at a constant simmer. Lift out onto a dish or pan, untie and spoon into bowls.

STRAWBERRY SHORTCAKE

The shortcake controversy baffles me. There is just one way to make it, and that is with a true shortcake. The substitution of a regular cake results in a strawberry topped cake. Here's how we've been making it for over a hundred years (except for one renegade aunt who shall remain nameless).

THE SAUCE
¾ *quart strawberries out of 1 quart*
½ *cup sugar*
1 *teaspoon lemon juice*

Cap berries, having set aside ¼ of the finest. Wash, drain and mash. Mix with sugar and lemon juice and cook over low heat until you have a sauce. This will not take long, so watch carefully and stir. Correct amount of sugar, as berries vary in sweetness. Set aside.

THE SHORTCAKE

3 *cups flour*   ¼ *pound softened butter*
½ *teaspoon salt*   ⅓ to ½ *cup milk*
2 *tablespoons sugar*

Preheat oven to 350°.

Sift flour, salt and sugar together. Cut in softened butter with a pastry blender. Add just enough of the milk to make a dough that is pliable, but not sticky. Using a floured board, roll dough out about 1″ thick. You may make one large biscuit or smaller, individual ones.

Place on a greased cookie sheet. Bake the large one for 20 minutes, the individual ones for 10. Cool, split through the center.

THE TOPPING
¼ *quart choice strawberries*
whipped cream

Stem, wash and drain berries. Split them in half. Whip cream.

TO SERVE

Put sauce between the layers of the biscuits, add whipped cream on top and the split berries.

OUR RICE PUDDING

A beloved dessert for at least two centuries, rice pudding seems unjustly neglected in this country today, although still a favorite with Europeans.

For 6 people.

> 1 *cup cooked rice (about ⅓ cup raw; ½–1 cup raw*
> *processed)*
> 2 *large or 3 small eggs*
> ½ *cup sugar*
> 2 *cups milk*
> ⅛ *teaspoon salt*
> 1 *teaspoon vanilla*
> *gratings of nutmeg*
> ½ *cup raisins*

Preheat oven to 325°.

Cook rice and steam until fluffy. Let cool. Beat eggs until very light and fluffy, adding sugar and continuing to beat. Add milk and seasonings, mix in raisins and rice.

Pour into lightly greased 1½-quart baking dish, set in a pan of warm water and bake in a moderate (325°) oven for 40 to 45 minutes or until a knife inserted in the center comes out clean.

Serve hot or cold. A spoonful of jelly on top is delightful.

GRANDFATHER'S COTTAGE PUDDING

My grandfather never cooked in his life, but this was his favorite dessert which he wanted every day for lunch. I figure he got his way about 60 of his 86 years. Serve with hot custard sauce (p. 161) or hot vanilla sauce (p. 160).

For 6 people.

> *6 apples or peaches or combination*
> *1 tablespoon lemon juice*
> *2 pats of butter*
> *¼ cup butter*
> *½ cup sugar*
> *1 lightly beaten egg*
> *1 cup flour*
> *1 teaspoon baking powder*
> *½ cup milk*

Preheat oven to 350°.

Peel and slice fruit fairly thin. Pour lemon juice over it. Melt the two pats of butter in an 8 x 8 x 2″ square pan. Spread the fruit evenly over the bottom, being sure it is well covered.

Cream ¼ cup butter and sugar until light and fluffy, then add lightly beaten egg. Sift flour and baking powder together, then add alternately with the milk to the creamed butter and sugar, beating well after each addition until you have a smooth batter. Pour over the fruit, but do not stir. Bake in moderate (350°) oven for about 40 minutes or until browned and done.

SNOW PUDDING

You might well expect this to be a New England recipe, but our Maryland snow pudding is so much better than the gelatinous types. When my mother was about eight, she was fascinated one day watching her Cousin Ethel create this frothy, ethereal looking delicacy. It soon became a favorite and still is.

For 6 people.

> *vanilla wafers or ladyfingers*   *½ cup sugar, scant*
> *2 cups water + 2 tablespoons*   *½ cup lemon juice*
> *5 tablespoons cornstarch*   *whites of 2 large or 3 small eggs*
> *½ teaspoon salt*   *custard sauce (p. 161)*

Line a 1½-quart mold or individual ones with the wafers or split ladyfingers. Try crushing the wafers on the bottom of the mold for a change.

Bring the 2 cups of water to a boil in a heavy saucepan. Sift the cornstarch, salt and sugar together and moisten with the 2 remaining tablespoons of water. Stir the cornstarch mixture rapidly into the boiling water and cook over low heat until thick and clear, stirring constantly, about 10 to 15 minutes. Add lemon juice.

Beat egg whites until stiff. Pour the hot cornstarch mixture into them slowly, blending carefully. Pour into the mold and set in refrigerator to chill well.

Serve with cold custard sauce.

LEMON CAKETOP PUDDING

If you're like me with a lifetime of letdowns when you taste the luscious looking dessert from a restaurant cart or bakery window, you'll doubly appreciate this pudding of Mother's. Someday I am going to make one, close the doors and eat it all up myself!

For 6 people.

> 2 *tablespoons butter*
> 1½ *cups sugar*
> ⅓ *cup flour*
> ¼ *teaspoon salt*
> ½ *cup lemon juice*
> 1 *tablespoon grated lemon peel*
> 3 *eggs, separated*
> 1¼ *cups milk*

Preheat oven to 375°.

Soften butter and cream with sugar. Add flour, salt, lemon juice and lemon peel. Beat egg yolks and mix with milk. Add to other ingredients. Beat egg whites stiffly and fold in. Pour into a flat-bottomed 1½-quart baking dish or 6 individual custard molds. Set in a pan of warm water and bake in the moderate (375°) oven for approximately 50 minutes.

Test for doneness with a knife blade. When the blade comes out clean, the pudding is done. Serve warm or cold.

GRANDMOTHER'S HUCKLEBERRY PUDDING

You may substitute blueberries, but the huckleberry has more flavor. We used to pick them ourselves, and that does make a world of difference. Serve with hard sauce and a hot lemon or rum sauce (p. 160).

For 6 people.

1½ *cups berries*	½ *teaspoon salt*
1½ *cups flour*	3 *teaspoons baking powder*
¼ *cup butter*	½ *cup milk*
½ *cup sugar*	1 *teaspoon vanilla*
1 *lightly beaten egg*	

Preheat oven to 350°.

Dredge berries in ½ cup of the flour. Cream the butter and sugar together. Beat egg lightly and add salt. Add to butter mixture. Sift remaining cup of flour with the baking powder and add alternately with the milk to the batter. Add vanilla. This is prepared like a cake batter and should be smooth.

Add berries by folding in gently. Pour into a well-greased 1½-quart pudding or 5x9″ loaf pan and bake in the moderate (350°) oven for 35 to 45 minutes until a cake tester comes out clean. Cool 10 minutes on a rack before removing from pan.

May be served hot or cold.

CAPE COD MOLASSES PUDDING

It's little wonder molasses appears so much in New England dishes, as it was the basis of their large and profitable rum business. As far back as 1670, they began to import molasses from the West Indies, distilling it in ever-increasing quantities. At that time rum was called variously Barbadoes liquor, rumb, rhym, rumbullion and kill-devil. As it became more and more plentiful, it also became cheaper and cheaper.

The Yankee traders by the early 18th century began to search for new markets and quickly found one in the infamous triangle trade. Molasses flowed into their harbors as regularly as the tide.

And it found its way into more than puddings, as the anything-but-abstemious New Englanders created myriad homebrews such as this incredible Salem one called "whistle-belly-vengeance": sour beer simmered in a kettle, sweetened with molasses and thickened with brown breadcrumbs, then drunk hot. No wonder they saw witches.

This is a straightforward pudding typical of the 18th and 19th centuries, although I imagine a spot of rum was probably added in the early days, and still could be if desired. It is fairly light and the least rich of the puddings. Serve with whipped cream, hard sauce or vanilla sauce (pp. 161 and 160).

For 6 to 8 people.

1 *well-beaten egg*	½ *cup raisins*
½ *cup dark molasses*	1 *cup flour*
½ *cup milk*	1 *teaspoon soda*
2 *tablespoons butter*	

Beat egg until frothy. Add molasses and milk, continuing to beat. Melt the butter and beat in. Add raisins. Sift the flour with the soda and mix into the batter until smooth.

To steam: Pour into a greased 1-quart pudding mold, which should be no more than ⅔ full. Cover mold tightly and place on a rack in a kettle over at least an inch of boiling water. Cover kettle tightly and let steam for 1 hour. Start with boiling water, then lower the heat to keep a constant simmering. Add more boiling water occasionally as it evaporates. (Pour it down the sides of the kettle, not over the pudding mold, and not above the level of the rack.)

After steaming, let the pudding sit in the mold without the cover for a few minutes before unmolding. Serve hot.

SWEET POTATO PUDDING

For 3 or 4 people.

>   ¾ *cup mashed sweet potato*
> ⅓ *cup sugar*
> *dash salt*
> 1 *egg, beaten*
> 1 *cup milk*
> 1 *teaspoon vanilla*
> 1 *tablespoon butter*
> *grating of nutmeg*
> *sliced pineapple*

Preheat oven to 350°.

Bake sweet potatoes until done. Discard skins and beat potatoes until creamy, adding sugar and salt. Beat egg, add milk and vanilla. Pour into sweet potato mixture, add butter and beat until smooth. Grate nutmeg to taste. Correct amount of sugar, as sweet potatoes vary in sweetness.

Pour into an 8x8x2″ buttered baking dish or 1-quart casserole, place sliced pineapple on top. Set in a pan of warm water and bake in a moderate (350°) oven until set. A silver knife inserted in the center should come out clean.

May be served with whipped cream.

INDIAN PUDDING

An 18th century standby, this is Grandmother Clary's spicy version. It is better served hot and needs no sauce, although whipped cream is delicious with it.

For 8 to 10 people.

> 6 *tablespoons cornmeal*   1 *tablespoon cinnamon*
> 3 *tablespoons flour*   1 *cup dark molasses*
> ½ *teaspoon salt*   1 *cup raisins*
> 1 *teaspoon ginger*   4 *cups milk*

Preheat oven to 300°.

Sift dry ingredients (except raisins) together. Pour in molasses and mix well. Then stir in raisins. Bring 3½ cups of the milk just to the boil and stir in.

Grease a 2-quart deep baking dish and pour batter in. Bake for ½ hour. Then pour the remaining ½ cup of milk on top of the pudding, leaving it in a puddle, not mixing it in. Continue to bake for 1½ hours more.

The center will remain soft.

STEAMED CARROT PUDDING

This really should be called a goody-goody pudding or some such. The carrots and apples lose their distinctive personalities, blending into a delicate succulence that must be tasted to be believed. Not as rich as a plum pudding, lighter and more moist than a suet pudding, this creates a special niche of its own.

It needs no sauces, although you may use a hot lemon or brandy one (p. 160) or whipped cream.

For 6 to 8 people.

> ½ *cup grated carrots*
> ½ *cup grated apples*
> ½ *cup ground suet*
> ½ *cup sugar*
> ½ *teaspoon soda*
> ½ *cup flour*
> ½ *teaspoon salt*
> ½ *teaspoon grated nutmeg*
> ½ *teaspoon cinnamon*
> ¼ *teaspoon cloves*
> ¾ *cup buttermilk*
> 1 *cup raisins*
> ½ *cup chopped nuts (optional)*

Grate carrots and apples. Combine with suet. Sift all dry ingredients together and blend with carrot mixture. Add buttermilk and stir well. Add raisins and nuts if using. Grease 1-quart pudding mold and pour in. Cover mold tightly and steam 2½ hours as directed on page 169. Let the pudding sit in the mold without the cover for a few minutes before unmolding. Serve hot.

GRANDMOTHER CLARY'S SUET PUDDING

Don't be put off by the name; this is a delicate, delicious steamed pudding. Originally it was made with sour milk which is almost impossible to get, but buttermilk is just as good.

This will make enough to serve 8 or 10, but since you can freeze it and resteam in foil in a pudding mold for ½ an hour, don't hesitate to make it for fewer.

Serve with hard sauce, whipped cream or vanilla sauce. I prefer hard sauce flavored with rum (p. 161), which would have sent Grandmother Clary into shock!

Your butcher will probably give you the suet.

1 *cup finely chopped suet*
1 *cup buttermilk*
½ *cup dark molasses*
1 *cup raisins*
3 *cups flour*
½ *cup sugar*
2 *teaspoons soda*
1 *teaspoon cinnamon*
1 *teaspoon grated nutmeg*
1 *teaspoon cloves*

Mix suet, buttermilk and molasses. Dredge raisins with ½ cup of flour. Sift remaining ingredients together. Combine all ingredients and pour into a 1½-quart greased pudding mold. Cover mold tightly and steam 2½ hours as directed on page 169. Let the pudding sit in the mold without the cover for a few minutes before unmolding.

Serve hot.

PLUM PUDDING

The plum puddings used to hang in grandmother's pantry like so many little shrunken heads, waiting for Resurrection. It is enough to renew one's faith to discover that something so unlovely can produce such delectability. The puddings were made at least a month before Christmas to give them time to season. (I've used one left over from the year before—still delicious).

This recipe will make enough for you and for presents. Plum puddings ship without any special care—just wrap and mail.

Allow about ½ cup per person when putting mixture into their bags; as they are so rich, most folk want only a small portion.

Makes enough for 16 to 18 people.

> 2 *pounds suet*
> 9 *eggs*
> 1 *pound sugar*
> 9 *tablespoons flour*
> ¼ *teaspoon salt*
> 1 *tablespoon cinnamon*
> 1 *teaspoon ground cloves*
> ½ *teaspoon allspice*
> 3 *ounces each orange and lemon peel*
> 4 *ounces each figs and dates*
> 2 *pounds currants*
> 3 *pounds dark raisins*
> 1 *pound citron*
> ½ *pound candied fruits, mixed and chopped fine*
> 1½ *quarts milk*
> 1½ *loaves dry, finely broken white bread*
> *unbleached muslin*

Cut suet very fine. Beat eggs and sugar until creamy, then mix with suet. Sift flour, salt and spices together, then sift over fruit, coating it well. Mix milk and broken bread together. Add to egg, sugar and suet mixture. Stir in fruit and flour mixture, blending well.

To bag for cooking: Cut muslin into ample squares which will permit tieing the cloth with string into bags. You will never want to make a pudding of less than 2 cups, as it would be too small to steam well. The bags must be big enough to hold the mixture loosely to allow for swelling during cooking, so judge your squares accordingly. Wet the muslin, dust it inside with a little flour to cover completely, put your batter in loosely and tie bag securely, leaving string to hang it up with.

To cook: Place bags on rack in kettle of boiling water, cover and cook for 2 hours. If you make larger bags, increase time to 4 hours. Be sure that the puddings are covered with water the entire time. Remove, hang up and let dry thoroughly. Hang them in your pantry or freeze them until ready to use.

To reheat for serving: Put on a rack in a kettle over (not in) boiling water, cover and steam until hot and soft. A small pudding for 4 will take about 40 minutes to an hour; a large pudding will take 2 hours.

To serve: Use a suitable silver or crystal plate and put steaming hot pudding in the center. At Christmas, I decorate the plate with holly or whatever is handy. Pour brandy over it, and set aflame. Serve with Hard Sauce (page 161) and one of the hot sauces (page 160).

TIPSY PUDDING

An old family favorite, this can be planned, but it has traditionally been the salvation of a tired bit of cake or a cake that just never got iced.

Pour sherry over the cake, enough to soak it. Pour custard sauce (p. 161) on top and stick in the refrigerator. Serve as is, with additional custard or with whipped cream.

APPLE DUMPLINGS

Use June apples, then Rome, Winesap, McIntosh or Greenings. For a sweeter dumpling, try Grimes Goldens. Whatever kind you use, this is a wonderful dessert. Serve it hot or cold with hot or cold custard sauce (p. 161).

For 6 dumplings.

THE FILLING

4½ cups apples, pared and sliced thin
1 teaspoon cinnamon
¾ cup sugar
2 tablespoons lemon juice
gratings of nutmeg

Prepare apples and combine with other ingredients. Set aside while you prepare the dough.

THE PASTRY DOUGH

2 cups flour
4 teaspoons baking powder
½ teaspoon salt
2 tablespoons sugar
⅓ cup vegetable shortening plus 1 tablespoon
¾ cup milk

Sift flour, baking powder, salt and sugar together. Work the shortening in with a fork or pastry blender until crumbly. Add milk gradually to make a soft dough, mixing with a fork. Knead gently two or three turns, then roll out on a floured board to ¼″ thickness. Cut into 5″ rounds or squares.

THE TOPPING

3–4 tablespoons melted butter
additional sugar

Melt butter and have ready.

Preheat oven to 425°.
Grease a flat baking pan. Put the seasoned fruit into the middle of each round or square of dough, distributing it equally among them. Moisten the edges of the dough with water and pinch it together around the fruit, making a dumpling.

Place the dumplings carefully in the pan. Spread the melted butter over them, then sprinkle lightly with the sugar. Add a small amount of boiling water to the pan, just enough to cover the bottom.

Bake the dumplings in hot (425°) oven for 10 minutes until slightly browned. Reduce heat to 350° and bake until done, about 45 minutes.

APPLE CRISP

There is just no apple crisp like this one. I know, because I tried many different recipes before I finally got the family's. Use good, tart apples.

For 6 people.

> *apples, thinly sliced, to make 4½ cups*
> *2 tablespoons lemon juice*
> *several gratings of nutmeg*
> *1¼ teaspoons cinnamon*
> *⅓ cup butter*
> *½ cup flour*
> *pinch of salt*
> *1 cup sugar*
> *3 tablespoons water*

Preheat oven to 350°.
Peel, core and thinly slice apples into a greased 8 x 8 x 2″ baking dish or 9″ deep dish pie plate, pour lemon juice over them, sprinkle with nutmeg and ¼ teaspoon cinnamon. Let stand.

Soften butter and cream with flour and salt. Add sugar, mix until crumbly. Add 1 teaspoon cinnamon and mix.

Pour water over the apples. Spread the butter mixture over the top pressing it down with your fingers to form a crust over the apples, covering them to the edge. Bake in the moderate (350°) oven for 35 minutes. Test the apples for doneness.

May be served with whipped cream or ice cream.

MOTHER'S DO-AHEAD AND STORE PIECRUST

Since the most irksome part of making piecrust is all the sifting and such, this is a boon. It will keep for several months in a tightly closed glass or plastic container right in your cupboard (not too hot a spot) and it is not only better but more economical than the commercial mixes. This will make about nine 9″ crusts when rolled thin as we do it. If you're a devotee of thicker crusts, it won't stretch as far.

10 cups flour (2½ pounds)
1¼ tablespoons salt
½ cup dry milk
4 cups shortening

Sift flour, salt and dry milk together in a large bowl. Cut in the shortening with a pastry blender or two knives until you have a crumbly mixture with the texture of coarse cornmeal. Store.

TO USE
For each 9″ crust
Measure out 1¼ cups of the mix and add 2 to 2½ tablespoons of icewater. Mix with a fork until the dough is like a rag and leaves the sides of the bowl. Squeeze together. Flour a board and roll out the dough, handling as little as possible, and rolling

from center out to form as round a crust as possible. Proceed with the individual recipe.

To make piecrust shells for individual servings as with apple-sauce, put dough over up-ended custard cups, shaping it to conform to the cup, place on a cookie sheet and bake in a pre-heated hot (450°) oven for about 12 minutes.

APPLE PIE

I've almost learned not to ask my husband what he wants for dessert, since his answer is invariably apple pie unless the blue-berries are in season.

For a 9" pie.

>5–6 *cups sliced, tart apples*
>2 *tablespoons lemon juice*
>½ *to* ¾ *cup sugar*
>1 *teaspoon cinnamon*
>½ *teaspoon nutmeg*
>1 *tablespoon cornstarch*
>*butter*
>*piecrust (p. 177)*

Use good, hard apples. Peel, core and slice thin. Pour lemon juice over them and stir. Add sugar to taste, then spices and corn-starch. Let stand.

Preheat oven to 425°, first covering its bottom with foil to catch spillage which is a mess to clean up.

Prepare piecrust and line pan. Put in apples and dot with butter. Top with the second crust, being sure edges of both crusts meet. Take a fork and press them together into a secure ruffle all around to get a good seal. Trim neatly. Pierce the crust to allow the steam to escape in cooking.

You may use a latticework crust, of course, which is simply strips of dough laid across the top, sealed to the bottom crust on each end. This is a great out when you're running low on piecrust dough.

Bake for 10 minutes in 425° oven. Reduce heat to 375° and continue to bake 45 more minutes. Serve hot or cold, with or without ice cream.

My husband is a purist, but I rather like a cup of raisins tossed in with the apples occasionally.

GRANDMOTHER'S PEACH MERINGUE PIE

This was always made with canned peaches, and it is just great.

For a 9" pie.

THE FILLING
3½ cups peaches
½ cup peach juice
1 tablespoon cornstarch
2 tablespoons sugar
pinch of salt
½ teaspoon almond extract
piecrust (p. 177)

Drain and mash peaches. Cook the juice with cornstarch until clear and thick, stirring constantly. Mixed into the mashed fruit. Add sugar, salt and almond extract. Taste and correct amount of sugar if necessary.

Preheat oven to 425°.

Prepare piecrust for bottom only and line pie pan.

Pour the peach filling into the piecrust and bake for 10 to 12 minutes in hot (425°) oven. Reduce temperature to 325° and bake for another 30 minutes. Remove from oven and let cool while you make meringue.

THE MERINGUE
3 frothily beaten egg whites
¼ teaspoon cream of tartar
6 tablespoons sugar
½ teaspoon vanilla

Preheat oven to 300°.

Beat egg whites until frothy, beating in cream of tartar. Gradually beat in the sugar until mixture is stiff and shiny. Add vanilla. Spread the meringue on the cooled pie getting it completely out to the edge so that it hits the crust and can seal to it.

Put pie in the 300° oven for 10 to 12 minutes or until meringue is golden brown.

GRANDMOTHER CLARY'S BLUEBERRY PIE

Grandmother Clary loved to tell this story about her old cook, Mrs. Packard, who was then about 70. It seems that Mrs. Packard was normally in the kitchen by 6 o'clock, attacking the floor with a mop as though it were a scourge to get shet of. One day, however, she just couldn't push the mop and complained of feeling poorly with a mysterious ailment she refused to discuss.

Finally, Grandmother Clary decided to ask old Dr. Hayes to come up the mountain to see about this ailment. When he repaired to the kitchen to talk to Mrs. Packard, Grandmother's curiosity overcame her and she hid behind a door to listen.

The patient refused to let Dr. Packard examine her, informing him that she was afraid her womb had fallen.

"Landsakes, woman," exclaimed Dr. Hayes," it's long since dried up and blown away!"

Mrs. Packard never complained again and was back in the kitchen baking blueberry pies the next day.

For a 9" pie.

4 *cups blueberries*
2 *tablespoons lemon juice*
¾ *cup sugar or to taste*
½ *teaspoon salt*
2½ *tablespoons tapioca*
½ *teaspoon cinnamon (optional)*
piecrust (p. 177)

Wash and pick over blueberries. Pour lemon juice over them, add sugar and salt. Stir in tapioca and cinnamon if used. Set aside for 15 minutes.

Prepare piecrust and line pie pan. Cover the oven bottom with foil to catch spillage as blueberries are the worst mess of all to clean up.

Preheat oven to 425°.

Fill piecrust and cover with a second crust as directed on page 178. Prick it. Set pie pan on the center rack of the preheated oven. Bake for 10 minutes. Turn heat down to 375° and bake for 30 minutes.

You may use this recipe for other berries also, if you wish.

CHERRY PIE

For a 9" pie.

1 *quart pitted cherries*
1 *cup sugar*
1 *tablespoon cornstarch*
⅛ *teaspoon salt*
nutmeg
butter
piecrust (p. 177)

Stew the cherries with ½ cup of the sugar for a few minutes until the juice flows. Drain, reserve juice and set cherries aside.

Combine the juice with the remainder of the sugar, the cornstarch and salt and cook over low heat until transparent and thickened, stirring occasionally. Add the cherries and grate the nutmeg over them.

Preheat oven to 425°. Line bottom with foil against spillage.

Prepare piecrust and line pan. Pour cherries into it, dot with butter and cover with a second crust as directed on page 178. Pierce it.

Bake for 10 minutes in hot (425°) oven, then turn heat down to 350° and continue to bake for another 35 minutes.

SOUR CREAM PIE

Milking time in the great barn at Snow Farm was a sensual symphony as comforting as curling up together in a warm bed. The soprano pings of the milk first hitting the pails were a staccato introduction to the muted rhythm that followed as the pails foamed full. The lowing of the cows carried the melody with a mournfully peaceful cadence, while the warmth and fragrance of the milk shimmered in the air.

All a prelude to that first sip of sweetness our scientific world is saving us from.

Just as naturally as it arrived, it could sour and create another need for ingenuity. This is one way the sour cream was used. A rich, sweet pie with a rather crunchy quality, it should be served in small wedges after a fairly light meal.

For a 9″ pie.

> 1 *cup heavy cream*
> 1 *tablespoon lemon juice or vinegar*
> 2 *beaten eggs*
> 1 *cup sugar*
> ¾ *teaspoon cinnamon*
> ½ *teaspoon cloves*
> 1 *tablespoon flour*
> ¾ *cup raisins*
> *piecrust (p. 177)*

Sour the cream by adding 1 tablespoon of lemon juice or vinegar and letting stand about 5 minutes. Pasteurized cream will not sour naturally, but spoil.

Beat eggs well, then beat in the sugar until creamy. Add seasonings and flour, beating again. Blend in cream, add raisins.

Preheat oven to 350°.

Prepare piecrust for bottom only and line pie pan. Pour in filling, and bake for 50 to 60 minutes. Test with a silver knife for doneness. It should come out clean.

Serve hot or cold.

EGGNOG PIE

This is made with a very diluted eggnog, so you will have to judge how strong yours is and proceed accordingly. You may use an eggnog without spirits if desired.

For a 9″ pie.

THE CRUST
2 cups vanilla wafers
⅓ cup butter
grating of nutmeg or 1 teaspoon vanilla or 2 teaspoons rum

Preheat oven to 300°.

Crush vanilla wafers fine, melt the butter and mix. Grate the nutmeg and mix again, or add vanilla or rum as preferred. Press the mixture into a pie pan firmly. Bake in a slow (300°) oven for 15 minutes. Cool thoroughly.

THE FILLING
1¾ cups eggnog	*1 package gelatin*
1 beaten egg yolk	*¼ cup water*
½ cup sugar, scant	*2 beaten egg whites*
⅛ cup evaporated milk	*1 teaspoon vanilla*

Heat the eggnog in the top of a double boiler over hot, not boiling water. Beat the egg yolk well, then beat with ¼ cup of the sugar until lemon colored. Add the milk to the egg. Pour the hot eggnog into this mixture and return to double boiler.

Meanwhile, melt the gelatin in the water over low heat.

Continue to heat the eggnog mixture, beating it constantly, until it coats a spoon. Add the melted gelatin. Set aside to cool.

Beat the egg whites until stiff with the remaining ¼ cup of sugar and the vanilla. Fold into the cooled custard and pour into the cool crust. Chill until ready to serve.

CRANBERRY-RAISIN PIE

Cranberry bogs still dot the Cape, hundreds probably just as they were when the Puritans arrived to find the Indians feasting on their fruit. It was not many decades before the canny New Englanders were not only making pies and tarts, but shipping the berries to England.

At Snow Farm, cranberries grew in a small bog beside the Pond, just enough to supply the birds and the family. As soon as the bog began to harden with the frost, solidifying enough to support a bit of weight, the berries were hand picked and tucked away.

Today, I buy them in season and freeze them for later use.

This very old recipe gives you a sweet 'n' tart flavor.

For a 9" pie.

   2 *cups cranberries*
   1 *cup raisins*
   1 *teaspoon lemon juice*
   1 *tablespoon flour*
   1 *cup sugar*
   ½ *cup water*
   1 *teaspoon almond extract*
   piecrust (p. 177)

Finely chop cranberries and raisins together, preferably in a blender. Pour lemon juice over them and stir. Mix in flour. Combine sugar, water and almond extract. Mix all ingredients together.

Preheat oven to 425°.

Prepare piecrust and line pie pan. Pour in filling. Cover with another crust (as directed on page 178), pierce. Bake in hot (425°) oven for 10 minutes, then lower heat to 375° and bake an additional 30 minutes.

MACAROON PIE

This is yummy rich, particularly when topped with fresh whipped cream.

For a 9″ pie.

> 16 *saltines*
> 16 *chopped dates*
> ¼ *cup chopped pecans*
> ¼ *cup grated coconut*
> 4 *beaten egg whites*
> ½ *teaspoon baking powder*
> ⅛ *teaspoon cream of tartar*
> 1 *cup sugar*
> ½ *teaspoon vanilla extract*
> ½ *teaspoon almond extract*

Preheat oven to 300°.

Crush saltines and combine with dates, pecans and coconut. This may all be done at once in the blender. Your total volume should be about 1¾ cups.

Beat egg whites until foamy, add baking powder and cream of tartar, beating to blend. Beat sugar in until mixture is stiff. Add vanilla and almond extract. Fold nut mixture in carefully.

Fold into pie pan and bake in slow (300°) oven for 25 minutes.

SNOW FARM MINCEMEAT

Off the rambling, inconvenient old kitchen at the Farm, still sporting its iron spit and baking ovens in the enormous, shallow brick fireplace, was the "warm pantry." It was the kind of room most of us dream of today, with shelf upon shelf lining its walls and cupboard beside cupboard bracing its generous counters, creating enough room to store all the jars and crocks and cans anyone could collect.

Its deep zinc sink, big enough to soak a mighty ham or bathe a lusty child in, listed crazily under a window looking out over the cutting garden up toward the horse barn.

Here the canned corn, the beans and tomatoes, the beets and applesauce kept company with the crocks of pickles and jugs of tomato juice. Behind it was the "cold pantry" where frigid puffs of air sneaked through the cracks of the wide-planked floor to blue one's hands in a thrice. This was home for such comestibles as the mincemeat waiting in its stone jar for a piecrust.

Today, just tuck it in your refrigerator.

Makes enough for four 9" pies.

> 1½ *pounds of lean beef*
> 4 *cups tart, hard apples*
> 2 *cups raisins*
> 1 *cup citron*
> 1 *teaspoon salt*
> 2 *cups sugar*
> 1 *cup strong coffee*
> 1 *cup chopped suet*
> 1 *cup meat stock*
> 1 *tablespoon cloves*
> 1 *tablespoon cinnamon*
> 1 *tablespoon nutmeg*

Boil beef covered until tender. Allow to cool in its own liquor. Run through the meat chopper, reserving the liquor. You should have 2 cups of meat.

Chop peeled apples fine. Mix the meat, apples, raisins and citron well together. Add remaining ingredients using 1 cup of the meat liquor. Mix well and simmer covered 1 hour. Seal in hot, sterilized jars.

To make pie: Preheat oven to 450°, first lining the bottom with foil to catch spillage.

Prepare crust (see p. 177) for top and bottom of as many pies as you plan to bake. Line pie pan and pour in mincemeat. Pour in about ¼ cup of brandy or bourbon and stir around, if you want to add our Maryland touch. Cover with top crust as directed on page 178.

Bake for 10 minutes at 450°, then reduce heat to 350° and continue to bake for 30 minutes.

Serve warm with hard sauce, or cold with ice cream.

PUMPKIN (OR SQUASH) PIE

Pumpkins, the biggest squashes of them all, seem to have only two purposes—Hallowe'en faces and pies. But perhaps that's really all one can ask for as a meaning in life?

For two 9" pies.

> 3 *cups cooked, mashed pumpkin or winter squash*
> 2 *cups firmly packed dark brown sugar*
> ½ *teaspoon salt*
> 2 *teaspoons cinnamon*
> 1 *teaspoon nutmeg*
> 1 *teaspoon ginger*
> ½ *teaspoon cloves*
> 1 *cup heavy cream*
> 4 *well-beaten eggs*
> 4 *tablespoons brandy or bourbon (optional)*
> 2 *teaspoons vanilla (optional)*
> 1½ *cups chopped nuts (optional)*
> *piecrust (p. 177)*

Preheat oven to 425°.

Mix pumpkin with all dry ingredients. Mix cream with the beaten eggs. Add spirits or vanilla as desired. Combine with pumpkin and whip well until smooth. Add nuts if desired.

Line pie pans with crust and pour batter in. Bake in the preheated oven for about 45 minutes or until done. A silver knife inserted in the center should come out clean.

PEACH COBBLER

When the peaches began to come in, it seems to me we had them sliced for breakfast, whole for lunch and cooked up some way for dinner. The dread of my life at that point was a bushel to be peeled for canning, a chore that led me to complain that "my entire life was being wasted in the kitchen."

This is one of the "cooked-up" ways we adored then and still do.

For 6 people.

> *2 cups sliced peaches*
> *1¾ cups sugar*
> *¾ cup flour*
> *pinch of salt*
> *2 teaspoons baking powder*
> *½ cup milk*
> *¼ teaspoon almond extract*
> *1 stick butter*

Preheat oven to 350°.

Slice peaches and mix with ¾ cup sugar. Let stand 2 hours.

Sift flour, salt and baking powder together, mix with 1 cup of sugar. Stir in milk and add almond extract.

Melt the butter in a deep baking dish and pour the batter over it. Do not stir. Pour the peaches over the top of the batter to form a layer.

Bake in a moderate (350°) oven for 50 to 55 minutes. If you use a glass baking dish, bake at 325°. Check it, as you do not want the juices to caramelize.

Serve with whipped cream, if desired.

COUSIN ETHEL'S ORANGE SPONGE

A light dessert, particularly good after a heavy meal or in the summer, when it can be done in the morning and left to chill.

For 6 people.

> 1 *package gelatin*
> ¼ *cup water*
> 4 *egg yolks, well beaten*
> 1 *cup orange juice*
> *juice of 1 lemon and its grated rind*
> ⅔ *cup sugar*
> 4 *egg whites, stiffly beaten*
> *whipped cream*

Dissolve gelatin in the ¼ cup of water. Beat egg yolks well, add orange and lemon juice, grated rind and sugar, continuing to beat. Cook in a double boiler over gently simmering (*not* boiling) water until slightly thickened, stirring constantly.

Off heat, stir in the dissolved gelatin, blending thoroughly. Put in refrigerator to cool. When it begins to set, beat egg whites until stiff, fold in gently, and pour mixture into a mold.

Return to refrigerator and chill. Serve with whipped cream.

SNOW FARM BOILED CIDER APPLESAUCE

This applesauce is deliciously different. The apples should remain chunky, not be pureed. You'll need a big kettle. At the

Farm, they stored it in a stoneware crock in the back pantry where it got better every day. My husband used to love a bowlful or a dollop on buttered bread for his after-school treat.

Makes about 6 quarts.

> 1 *gallon sweet cider*
> 16 *pounds sweet apples (about 48 cups)*
> 3 *pounds sugar*
> 1 *cinnamon stick*

Boil cider down to 2 quarts. Meanwhile, peel, core and slice apples quite thin.

When cider has boiled down, put in as many apples as you can, the sugar and the cinnamon stick. Cover and cook very slowly without stirring until the apples are tender but not mushy. If you cannot get all the apples in at one time, as the first batch is done, remove it to a large bowl and add the uncooked ones to the cider syrup.

When all the apples are cooked, combine in the syrup and set aside overnight.

The next day, drain them. Boil the remaining syrup down until quite thick and pour again over the apples. Practically all the syrup should be absorbed, and you will have a thick, rich applesauce.

MAPLE SYRUP APPLESAUCE

Remember, you only get about half as much applesauce as you have apples to start with, so if you want to make a batch, double this. And remember, too, apples vary in their juiciness, so you must judge your liquid a bit. In this recipe, if in doubt as to juiciness of your apples, go shy on the water. You can always add it as they cook, if needed.

For 4 to 6 people.

about 3 pounds tart apples, to make 8 cups sliced
1 cup maple syrup
1 cup water
2 good slices of lemon
1 teaspoon cinnamon
several gratings of nutmeg

Peel, core and slice apples thin. In a heavy pot, combine maple syrup, water and lemon. Add apples. Cook covered at a low simmer about 35 minutes or until nice and squishy. Check occasionally and stir, so that they don't stick.

When done, add the cinnamon and nutmeg to taste. Mash the apples with a spoon. They will be nice and lumpy with a rich, bronzed color rather than the pallid, runny commercial type.

Serve alone or with custard sauce (p. 161) for dessert. Put into individual baked piecrust shells (see p. 178), add custard for a special treat. Or use as a condiment.

BAKED MAPLE APPLES

Bake as many as you wish. They may be served hot or cold, and will keep several days in the refrigerator. Use good, tart apples.

apples as desired
maple syrup
butter
cinnamon
gratings of nutmeg
lemon juice
brown sugar

Preheat oven to 325°.

Wash and core as many apples as desired. Pour them ⅔ full of maple syrup. Add about ½ a pat of butter to each. Dash cinnamon on each, then a grating of nutmeg and several drops of lemon juice. Top with several sprinkles of brown sugar.

Put water about ½″ deep in a baking pan just big enough to hold your apples, add ½ cup of maple syrup and brown sugar. Stir. Put apples into pan. Bake in the moderate oven until done. They will be soft and sweet when ready. The syrup can be used to pour over them.

CHARLOTTE RUSSE

A beautiful looking dessert, it's deliciously rich. Make it ahead for a luncheon or supper party.

For 10 to 12 people.

THE CRUST
sponge cake or ladyfingers
sherry

Have enough cake or ladyfingers to line the mold you plan to use. Soak them in sherry until well saturated and line a 3-quart mold, slicing cake about ½″ thick or splitting ladyfingers in half. Set aside.

THE FILLING
1 package gelatin
¼ cup water
1 cup milk
1 cup cream
4 egg yolks, beaten
5 tablespoons sugar
2 egg whites, beaten 'til light
1 cup whipping cream
2 teaspoons vanilla

Dissolve gelatin in the ¼ cup of water. Scald milk and cream together, then stir in the gelatin. Beat egg yolks well, then beat in sugar until creamy. Pour the hot milk mixture into the eggs very slowly, mixing well as you go along. Put into top of a double boiler and heat until the mixture coats a spoon.

Beat egg whites until very light, but not dry. Pour the custard mixture into them, folding gently until smooth. Chill until quite cold.

Whip cream and add vanilla. Fold into the chilled custard mixture, then pour into the cake-lined mold.

Refrigerate for several hours before serving.

BOURBON BALLS

These keep indefinitely in the refrigerator. Serve them after dinner with coffee and brandy or as you wish.

Makes about 60 or 70.

> 2¼ cups vanilla wafers (1 box)
> 2 teaspoons cocoa
> 1¼ cups chopped pecans
> 2 tablespoons dark corn syrup
> 8 tablespoons and a splash of bourbon
> dash of brandy
> dash of vanilla
> 1⅛ cups powdered sugar

Crush wafers very fine, mix with cocoa, then nuts. Add syrup, spirits and vanilla. Mix well with fingers until light and creamy. Form into small balls about the size of a marble and roll in the powdered sugar. Let stand about an hour, then refrigerate in jars until ready to serve.

Rum may be substituted for the bourbon.

CANDIED GRAPEFRUIT OR ORANGE RIND

Nothing useful ever went to waste, and this is how the citrus rinds were recycled. A good candy during the holidays, as its sweet-tart flavor makes a welcome relief from all the rich sweets.

6 grapefruit rinds or 12 orange or combination
water
salt
2 cups sugar
⅓ cup light corn syrup
1 cup water
additional sugar

Remove pulp from rinds. Soak them overnight in water. Drain. Using enough fresh, cold water to cover, add 1 teaspoon salt and the rinds. Bring to a boil. Pour off the water.

Repeat this process 3 times or until the bitter flavor is gone.

Put rinds in fresh water and boil again until tender, covered. Drain. Cut into narrow strips about ⅛ to ¼″ thick.

Make a syrup by boiling the sugar, syrup and 1 cup of water together until you can spin a thread from a spoon. Add the sliced fruit and simmer until transparent.

Drain. Roll the rind in the additional sugar until coated. Spread out and allow to dry before storing.

COOKIES AND CAKES

SAND TARTS

My big brother always used to say to grandmother, "Mammy, please make me some sand tarts!" These are wafer-thin, crisp and well worth the trouble they take.

Makes about 140 cookies, 1½" in diameter.

> 1 *cup butter*
> 2 *cups sugar*
> 2 *separated eggs*
> 3 *cups flour*
> ½ *teaspoon nutmeg or mace*
> 1 *teaspoon soda*
> *melted butter*
> *canister of ⅓ cinnamon and ⅔ sugar*
> *blanched, split almonds*

Cream butter and sugar together until light and fluffy. Beat egg yolks and whites separately and well. Add the yolks to the butter mixture and mix well. Add the whites and again mix. Sift the flour, nutmeg or mace and soda together. Mix into the butter mixture and blend thoroughly.

Roll the dough into thin rolls about 1½" in diameter, wrap in foil and chill.

Preheat oven to 400°.

Grease cookie sheet. Slice dough paper thin and place on sheet. Brush each cookie with melted butter, then sprinkle the cinnamon-sugar over it and press an almond in the center.

Bake for about 10 minutes, watching closely as they burn in a wink.

ALMOND RINGS

My old recipe says, "These'll last forever if you don't eat them." But they're hard to keep around. My husband, who professes to dislike sweets, disposed of a dozen in about 8 minutes the first time I made them for him.

Makes about eighty 2 to 3″ rings.

> ¾ *pound butter*
> ½ *pound sugar*
> 3 *separated eggs*
> 4 *cups flour*
> 1½ *teaspoons vanilla or lemon juice*
> 2 *teaspoons cinnamon*
> ¼ *cup sugar*
> ¼ *cup powder-fine chopped almonds or walnuts*

Preheat oven to 400°.

Cream butter and sugar until light and fluffy. Separate eggs and beat yolks lightly. Mix with the butter and sugar. Add the flour and vanilla or lemon juice. Mix well.

Mix cinnamon, ¼ cup sugar and nuts together. Beat egg whites lightly. Grease cookie sheets.

Using a lightly floured board, roll the dough out thin. Cut into strips 1″ wide or less and cut or break them off into 3″ lengths. Working as lightly as possible, press ends together with your fingers and flatten into more-or-less ring shapes. (A lot easier than cutting out rings and rerolling leftover dough each time.) Brush tops with egg whites, then sprinkle with the nut mixture.

Bake for 8 to 10 minutes, watching closely.

GINGER COOKIES

This is how we made them in Southern Maryland a hundred years ago, and it's still the better way.

Makes about 152 cookies 2″ in diameter.

> 1 *pound butter (2 cups)*
> 1 *pound brown sugar (2¼ cups)*
> ¼ *cup dark molasses*
> 1 *beaten egg*
> ¾ *pound flour (3 cups)*
> 4 *tablespoons ground ginger*

Cream butter and brown sugar until light. Add molasses and the well-beaten egg, mixing thoroughly. Sift flour and ginger together, then mix into the butter mixture well. Put the dough into the icebox to chill for several hours.

Preheat oven to 400°.

Flour board well. Take out only as much dough as you can roll at one time. It should be stiff, so that you do not need much additional flour. Roll dough fairly thin, cut with cookie cutter. Place on greased cookie sheets and bake for 8 to 10 minutes.

ICEBOX COOKIES

Handy cookies because you can bake some one day and keep the remainder of the dough to bake another day.

Makes about 130 cookies 2″ in diameter.

> 1 *cup brown sugar*
> 1 *cup granulated sugar*
> 1 *cup butter*
> 2 *well-beaten eggs*
> 1 *teaspoon vanilla*
> 3½ *cups flour*
> 1 *teaspoon soda*
> 1 *teaspoon cinnamon*
> 2 *cups chopped nuts*

Combine sugars. Cream butter until light, then cream with the sugar. Beat eggs well and blend into butter mixture. Add vanilla. Sift the flour with the soda and cinnamon and mix in well. Stir in the chopped nuts.

Shape into rolls about 1½″ in diameter, wrap well in foil and refrigerate for 24 hours.

Preheat oven to 400°.

Slice cookies off the roll very thin. Grease cookie sheet and place on it. Bake in hot (400°) oven about 10 minutes or until turning golden. Cool and store in airtight containers.

SOUR CREAM COOKIES

These are a real old-fashioned New England plain cookie. They have a good substantial quality about them, are easy to bake since they don't require the watchful eye a short cookie does.

Makes about 100 cookies 2″ in diameter.

> ¾ *tablespoon lemon juice or vinegar*
> ¾ *cup cream*
> 1 *beaten egg*
> 1 *cup sugar*
> 2 *cups flour*
> ¼ *teaspoon soda*
> 1½ *teaspoons baking powder*
> ¼ *teaspoon salt*
> ¼ *teaspoon nutmeg*
> *additional sugar*

Preheat oven to 350°.

Add lemon juice or vinegar to the cream and set aside for 5 minutes to sour. Beat egg well, gradually beat in sugar and then soured cream.

Sift the dry ingredients together. Mix into the egg. Grease a cookie sheet and drop the batter by teaspoonfuls on it, leaving

about an inch between each one, as these cookies spread out.
Sprinkle with some sugar.

Place on the center rack in moderate (350°) oven and bake.
When cool, store in an airtight container.

ENGLISH MATRIMONIALES

A traditional wedding sweet, these will make high tea or any
other time memorable.

Makes about 1½ dozen.

> 1¼ cups flour
> 1 cup brown sugar, firmly packed
> 1¼ cups rolled oats
> ½ teaspoon salt
> ¾ cup softened butter
> ¾ cup raspberry jam

Preheat oven to 325°.

Mix flour, sugar, oats, salt and softened butter together until
you have a crumbly mass. Grease a shallow 6 x 9″ baking pan and
spread half of the mixture over the bottom, pressing it down
firmly. Cover with the jam. Sprinkle the remainder of the flour
mixture over the top and press down firmly.

Bake in moderate (325°) oven for 40 to 45 minutes. When
cool, cut into squares.

RUSSIAN TEACAKES

Rich confections, this recipe infiltrated the family about three
generations ago via a Texas wife. I give little baskets of them for
Christmas presents with enormous success. Don't try to keep
these over a month.

Makes about 130 little cakes.

> 1 cup butter
> ½ cup sifted powdered sugar
> 2 cups sifted flour
> 1 cup pecans, chopped powder fine
> 1 teaspoon vanilla
> additional powdered sugar

Preheat oven to 300°.

Cream butter and sugar together until fluffy. Gradually mix in flour, then nuts, then vanilla, until completely blended. Roll dough with your fingers into cherry-size balls. Grease a cookie sheet and bake them in moderate (300°) oven for about 30 minutes. They should be just faintly golden.

When they have cooled somewhat, roll them in the additional sugar to coat them. Store between layers of waxed paper.

MACAROONS

Mother's perfect little sweets.

Makes about 2 dozen.

> 3 frothily beaten egg whites
> 1 cup almond paste
> 1 cup sifted powdered sugar
> ½ teaspoon almond extract

Preheat oven to 250°.

Beat egg whites until quite frothy. Mix the almond paste into them, then blend in the powdered sugar. Add the almond extract.

Cover a flat cookie sheet with buttered wax paper. Drop the mixture on it in small rounds about the size of a nutmeg. Bake in slow (250°) oven until a light brown, checking carefully so they do not burn.

Remove from the paper immediately.

APPLESAUCE CAKE

Since the Snows raised some of the finest apples in New England, you'd think they'd have made a better applesauce cake than our Southern Maryland one. Not so. This is a Moss family recipe.

1 *cup butter*
2 *cups sugar*
2 *cups applesauce*
2 *teaspoons soda*
1 *teaspoon cinnamon*
1 *teaspoon allspice*
1 *teaspoon salt*
3½ *cups flour*
2 *cups chopped raisins*
¼ *cup chopped citron*

Preheat oven to 350°.

Cream butter and sugar well. Combine applesauce and soda. Add to the creamed butter. Sift the spices and salt with the flour. Add to the applesauce mixture, mixing well.

Have your raisins and citron chopped fine. Mix into the batter thoroughly.

Grease a 5 x 9″ loaf pan and pour in the batter. Bake in moderate (350°) oven for 45 minutes or until done. Cake will leave the sides of the pan when done.

MAPLE SYRUP CAKE

A delicately flavored, not too rich cake, it is good as is, but better with whipped cream or ice cream. It may be iced with a caramel or maple sugar icing.

1½ *cups flour*
½ *teaspoon salt*
2 *teaspoons baking powder*
1 *tablespoon softened butter*
1 *beaten egg yolk*
¾ *cup maple syrup*
6 *tablespoons milk*
1 *teaspoon vanilla*

Preheat oven to 350°.

Sift flour, salt and baking powder together. Have butter softened to the melting point, but not hot. Beat egg yolk and add the butter, maple syrup and milk to it in that order, beating thoroughly as you go.

Mix the sifted dry ingredients into the egg mixture. Add the vanilla and mix well.

Grease and flour an 8″ square cake pan. Pour in the batter and bake in moderate (350°) oven for 25 minutes.

EASTERN SHORE DATE NUT LOAF

A rich date-nut concoction, our version falls more into the cake class than does Jean Snow's austere New England date nut bread (p. 126).

4 *well-beaten egg yolks*
1 *cup sugar*
1 *teaspoon vanilla*
1 *tablespoon brandy*
2 *cups dates*
2 *cups walnuts*
1 *cup flour*
¼ *teaspoon salt*
2 *teaspoons baking powder*
4 *stiffly beaten egg whites*

Preheat oven to 350°.

Separate eggs. Beat yolks until thick and creamy, then add sugar gradually, continuing to beat. Add vanilla and brandy.

Cut up dates, chop walnuts and mix together.

Sift dry ingredients together. Stir ½ of the dry mixture into the date-nut mixture, coating the dates thoroughly.

Stir the remaining dry ingredients into the egg yolk mixture. Then blend the two mixtures together into a batter.

Beat the egg whites until stiff and fold in gently.

Grease a 9½ x 5½ x 3″ loaf pan, line it with waxed paper to prevent the loaf from drying out. Bake in moderate (350°) oven for 1 hour and 15 minutes.

LADY BALTIMORE CAKE

Great-aunt Janie Revell Moss's version of this luscious, rich cake has been acknowledged by three generations as perfection. It was always the birthday cake for her children and grandchildren, as well as the cake for any special occasion.

THE CAKE
1 *cup butter*
2 *cups sugar*
2¾ *cups flour*
3 *teaspoons baking powder*
¼ *teaspoon salt*
1 *cup milk*
1½ *teaspoons almond extract*
6 to 8 *stiffly beaten egg whites*

Preheat oven to 350°.

Cream butter and sugar together until light. This may be done in a mixer, but the remainder of the batter should be mixed by hand. Sift flour, baking powder and salt together. Add alternately with the milk to the butter mixture, stirring thoroughly after each addition. Add the almond extract.

Beat egg whites until stiff but not dry. Fold them gently into the batter. Grease and flour 3 cake pans. Pour batter in them equally. Bake in moderate (350°) oven for 30 to 35 minutes or until done. Cakes will begin to leave sides of pans when done. Allow to cool on racks before icing.

FILLING AND ICING
2 cups English walnuts
2 cups raisins or figs or a combination
2 cups sugar
½ cup water
3 stiffly beaten egg whites
1 teaspoon vanilla

Chop nuts and fruit fine and mix together thoroughly. Boil the sugar and water together until the syrup spins a thread when dropped from a spoon.

Pour the syrup slowly over the stiffly beaten egg whites, beating constantly as you do. Then add the vanilla and the nut mixture, blending thoroughly.

Spread over each layer and top.

DARK FRUITCAKE

For the past two generations, those who couldn't get home for Christmas always received a piece of home to cheer them . . . a plum pudding and two fruitcakes, redolent of brandy, one dark to please my brother, one light to delight me.

This is great-grandmother's recipe which has been used for almost 200 years that we know of, passed down by word of mouth and written down just a few years ago.

As soon as Thanksgiving was over, the kitchen became a frantic bakery. First the fruitcakes were made, as they needed to season. Every week they were given a little drink of brandy, then carefully rewrapped to hibernate. If you'll continue to give them a drink, they'll last 'til next year.

Makes one 10″ tube pan cake plus four 4½ x 8″ loaves—about 9 pounds.

> 1 *pound sugar*
> 1 *pound butter*
> 1 *dozen eggs*
> 1 *pound flour*
> 2½ *teaspoons baking powder*
> 1 *tablespoon cinnamon*
> 1 *teaspoon nutmeg*
> 1 *teaspoon ground cloves*
> 2 *pounds dark raisins*
> 2 *pounds currants*
> ¼ *pound seeded dates*
> ¼ *pound figs*
> 1 *pound citron*
> ½ *pound each candied pineapple and cherries*
> 3 *ounces each orange and lemon peel*
> 1 *cup chopped pecans or English walnuts*
> ¼ *cup brandy or port (or rum)*
> 1 *teaspoon vanilla*
> ½ *pint homemade strawberry preserves or grape jelly*

Preheat oven to 300°.

Cream sugar and butter until light and fluffy. Add the eggs one at a time, beating well after each. Sift all but ½ cup of the flour with the baking powder and spices, mix with butter.

Put raisins and currants in boiling water for about 5 minutes to puff them up. Drain. Chop coarsely dates, figs and citron. Chop pineapple and halve cherries. Combine with orange and lemon peel and the ½ cup of flour and be sure the fruit is well-dusted so it doesn't stick together. Mix into the batter well.

Chop nuts so they are in pieces, not bits. Add with brandy and vanilla. Mix well. Add preserves and mix again.

Line a 10″ tube cake pan plus four 4½ x 8″ loaf pans with

foil and pour in batter. Bake in slow (300°) oven for 4 hours. Check the smaller pans, with cake tester for doneness at 2½ hours. Turn cakes out of pans and cool on a cloth covered rack overnight.

Cool cake on a rack, put into foil, pour about a quarter cup brandy (or ½ brandy, ½ rum) over it, close tightly and over-wrap well in plastic, then put in a sealed tin. It must be airtight. Continue to pour brandy over it weekly.

BLACK FRUITCAKE

This is a simple, quite dark fruitcake. It was my great, great-aunt Mary Josephine Parkinson Moss's recipe. She belonged to what we used to call the Mosshaven branch of the family, after their home's name. Aunt Mary lived to be ninety some, and it was she, who in a fit of cleaning out when she was very old, threw away practically all her cookbooks and recipes. This one survived, as it had been copied.

Makes two 8″ tube cakes.

> ½ *cup butter*
> 1 *cup brown sugar*
> 1 *cup molasses*
> 3 *beaten eggs*
> 1 *cup milk*
> 1 *teaspoon nutmeg*
> 1 *teaspoon cinnamon*
> 1 *teaspoon allspice*
> 1 *teaspoon ground cloves*
> 1 *tablespoon brandy*
> 3 *cups sifted flour*
> 2½ *teaspoons baking powder*
> *pinch of salt*
> 1 *pound dark raisins*
> 1 *pound currants*
> ½ *pound chopped citron*
> ½ *pound blanched almonds*

Preheat oven to 325°.

Cream butter and sugar, add molasses, eggs, milk, spices and brandy, mixing well. Sift 2½ cups of the flour with baking powder and salt, mix well with butter mixture. Use remaining ½ cup flour to dust raisins, currants and citron to prevent stickiness, combine with almonds, then stir into batter. Grease and line two 8″ tube pans with waxed paper. Bake in slow (325°) oven for 2½ hours. Turn cakes out and cool on a cloth-covered rack overnight.

Wrap in foil and plastic wrap, place in sealed tin. You may also pour brandy over this version (see Dark Fruitcake, 204).

WHITE FRUITCAKE

This has always been my favorite fruitcake because it is so full of fruit, so moist and so rich it's almost a candy-cake.

Makes one 10″ tube pan cake plus two 3 x 5″ loaves.

> 1 *cup sugar*
> ¾ *cup butter*
> 2 *cups flour*
> ¼ *teaspoon soda*
> 1 *teaspoon salt*
> ½ *teaspoon cream of tartar*
> 1 *pound white raisins*
> 1 *pound chopped blanched almonds*
> ½ *pound chopped candied cherries*
> ¼ *pound chopped candied pineapple*
> ½ *pound chopped citron*
> ½ *cup fresh coconut (moist canned may be substituted)*
> 4 *tablespoons milk*
> 6 *well-beaten egg whites*

Preheat oven to 250°.

Cream sugar and butter together. Sift all dry ingredients except ½ cup of the flour together. Combine the chopped fruit and dust with the ½ cup of flour, trying to coat each piece. This permits the fruit to "float" better in the batter.

Add the fruit and coconut to dry ingredients, add milk and mix thoroughly. Fold in the beaten egg whites gently.

Grease your pans, then line with heavy brown paper and grease it. Fill your pans ¾ full. Place a small pan of water in the oven which will help to keep your cakes moist. Bake in the slow (250°) oven 3 hours for the large cake or until done. The small loaves should be checked for doneness with a cake tester after an hour and ten to twenty minutes. Be careful not to overcook, as the cake will dry out.

Remove from oven and place pans on a rack to cool for several hours. Place cloth on the rack and turn cakes out on it, letting remain overnight. The next morning prick tiny holes in the cake. Soak a cloth in brandy or bourbon and place cakes on them, put on a sheet of foil and pour brandy or bourbon over cake. Wrap cloth tightly around it, rewrap in the foil and in plastic and put in tightly covered box or container. Once a week, give it another drink.

BEVERAGES

FISH HOUSE PUNCH

This smooth and lethal punch came to me from my great-aunt Janie Revell Moss, a beautifully erect raconteur with white hair piled on top of her head, a black ribbon around her throat and a cigarette in her hand. (Her mother smoked cigarillos, but only in private.) It is reputedly a variant on the Old South River Club recipe which goes back into the 18th century. A true gentlemen's drink, it will make the unwary suddenly pass out at polite receptions, so do watch it.

Makes 8 gallons of punch which will yield 16 to 24 gallons when soda is added. Enough for 192 thirsty people to have a pint apiece, God help them.

> 8 *quarts of rye whiskey*
> 1 *quart Jamaican (black) rum*
> 1 *quart peach brandy*
> 5 *cups sugar*
> 2 *cups lemon juice*
> 1 *cup very strong tea*
> *soda water*

Pour liquors slowly over sugar until dissolved. Add lemon juice and tea. Strain through cheesecloth. (Originally, it was strained through absorbent cotton.) Store in a covered crock in a cool place or in the refrigerator for 4 weeks.

To serve: Add 1 to 2 quarts of soda for each quart of the

punch, according to your taste. Do use a cake of ice in the punch-bowl, not cubes as they dilute it too much.

I have kept this punch for 6 months, and it probably will keep a year.

BIG JOE'S EGGNOG

Big Joe is my father, and a finer judge of a good drink would be hard to find. He used to make the eggnog in a great crock a day or so before its first use. It mellows well, and can be kept in the refrigerator quite awhile. If there's any leftover, mix it with some whipped cream and freeze for a mousse.

For about 30 people.

> 2 *dozen separated eggs*
> 1¼ *pounds granulated sugar*
> 2½ *pints cream*
> 1 *quart brandy*
> 1 *quart dark rum*
> 2 *quarts milk*
> *grated nutmeg*

Separate eggs. Beat yolks until light and fluffy. Add sugar to them, beating until thick and creamy. Beat 1½ pints of the cream until thick.

Add the liquor slowly to the egg yolks, mixing well. Add the milk. Add the unbeaten pint of cream. Mix well. Add the beaten cream, stirring in gently. Beat the egg whites until stiff but not dry. Fold them into the mixture. Cover and chill.

This will be frothy. When ready to serve, you may stir the froth in a bit, if desired.

Use freshly grated nutmeg if possible on each cup.

MINT JULEPS

I can't ever remember living anywhere that Daddy didn't have a mint bed perfuming some spot. I wonder now if he tucked some roots in his pocket everytime we moved?

We always used it in our iced tea, of course, but the overwhelming moment was my first julep when I was seventeen.

Here is how we make them. Best served in the garden.

Pre-chill glasses.

Put 5 or 6 mint leaves in each, add a teaspoon of sugar and crush with a muddler.

Fill glasses with crushed ice straight from the freezer, so it is dry, not mushy. Return glasses to refrigerator and allow to frost, about ½ hour.

Stir in 1½ jiggers of bourbon. Add as much more crushed ice as needed; stir. Stick sprigs of mint in it.

Serve on a salver with a linen napkin. This is necessary for the comfort of the drinker as well as to preserve the frost.

Use silver sippers if you have them.

Index